10 TRUE TALES

P9-DNT-457

HEROES OF HURRICANE KATRINA

Allan Zullo

SCHOLASTIC INC.

To my dear friends and hurricane survivors, Mark and Ellen Starkman
and Michael and Ann Wechter, who are proof positive of the resiliency
of the human spirit.
—A. Z.

Copyright © 2015 by The Wordsellers, Inc.

All rights reserved. Published by Scholastic Inc., *Publishers since 1920.* SCHOLASTIC and associated logos are trademarks and/or registered trademarks of Scholastic Inc.

The publisher does not have any control over and does not assume any responsibility for author or third-party websites or their content.

No part of this publication may be reproduced, stored in a retrieval system, or transmitted in any form or by any means, electronic, mechanical, photocopying, recording, or otherwise, without written permission of the publisher. For information regarding permission, write to Scholastic Inc., Attention: Permissions Department, 557 Broadway, New York, NY 10012.

ISBN 978-0-545-83123-9

10 9 8 7 6 5 4 3   15 16 17 18 19/0

Printed in the U.S.A   40
First printing 2015

Book design by Cheung Tai

ACKNOWLEDGMENTS

I wish to thank the heroes featured in this book for their willingness to recall details, in personal interviews with me of the dramatic and sometimes emotional memories of their experiences during and immediately after Hurricane Katrina.

My appreciation extends to Angela H. Hirsch, former chief of the community relations division of the US Coast Guard Office of Public Affairs, and to Scott Price, deputy Coast Guard historian, who provided me with additional information and confirmation of certain facts.

CONTENTS

A Storm for the Ages VII

"Ain't Nobody Else Gonna Die" 1
Donald Colletti and Jimmy Pitre

"Will I Be Hoisting My Own Neighbors?" 21
Coast Guard Helicopter Pilot Craig O'Brien

"We'll Have to Shoot Our Way Out!" 39
Police Chief John Dubuisson

"We're Not Leaving Anyone Behind" 55
Michael and Carolyn Gerhold

"We're the Go-To Guys Now" 73
Ken Bellau, Earl Barthé, Jr., and the Soul Patrol

"It's Time to Save Some Lives" 96
Coast Guard Rescue Swimmer Laurence Nettles

"There's No Way We're Going to Drown" 115
Ashton Pruitt

"It's Like the End of Days" 127
Dr. Scott Delacroix

"I Must Rescue Those Animals" 146
Jane Garrison

"I Can't Let the People Down" 162
Brice Phillips

A STORM FOR THE AGES

Hurricane Katrina is considered the most catastrophic natural disaster in United States history.

The devastation was staggering: After Katrina slammed into the Gulf Coast, making landfall in Louisiana and Mississippi on August 29, 2005, it claimed more than 1,800 lives, ravaged entire beachside towns, drowned much of New Orleans, destroyed or made uninhabitable 300,000 homes, and left hundreds of thousands of victims homeless. The fierce storm swamped or flattened 90,000 square miles of land—nearly equal to the size of the United Kingdom—and caused more than $108 billion in damage. It also profoundly harmed the environment, causing oil and chemical spills totaling more than eight million gallons from ruptured storage tanks, damaged refineries, and busted pipelines.

The casualty figure would have been much worse if people hadn't heeded officials' pleas to evacuate. More than 1 million residents of southeastern Louisiana, including about 400,000

New Orleanians, fled before the storm. But nearly 100,000 people remained in the city. For various reasons, they, along with thousands across the Gulf Coast, preferred to ride out the storm in their homes. Some wanted to stay behind with loved ones and pets, while others wanted to protect their residences from possible looters.

Tens of thousands who lived near or below the poverty line in New Orleans couldn't leave because they didn't have cars or the money to cover the costs of evacuating, such as for food, lodging, and transportation. About 10,000 people found refuge ahead of time in the Superdome, an indoor stadium located on relatively high ground near downtown, that was designated by city officials as a "shelter of last resort."

The country's costliest hurricane made landfall near Buras, Louisiana, close to the mouth of the Mississippi River, at about 6 A.M. as a Category 3 storm, packing sustained winds of 127 miles an hour. As it roared up the eastern edge of the state, Katrina sideswiped New Orleans and laid waste to the Mississippi coastal towns of Waveland, Bay St. Louis, Pass Christian, Long Beach, Gulfport, and parts of Biloxi and Ocean Ridge.

Much of Katrina's destructive power came from its storm surge, the abnormal rise of water pushed ashore by the intensity of a hurricane's winds. The storm tide—the term for the heightened water level created by the combined storm surge and the normal tide—reached over 30 feet high along the coast, destroying most everything in its path and driving flood-waters inland for several miles.

Katrina's winds struck New Orleans with only a glancing blow, but the storm surge threw a knockout punch. The city, which lies an average of 6 feet below sea level, had been protected by a series of seawalls and levees. The storm surge not only overtopped the levees but also weakened several of them until more than 50 breaches burst open, unleashing a massive deadly flood that spread throughout 80 percent of the city.

As water gushed into low-lying neighborhoods and rose to the ceilings of their houses, people scrambled to attics and rooftops for safety. Others were marooned in flooded hospitals, stores, hotels, and apartment buildings. Many, sadly, were unable to escape and drowned, accounting for about 40 percent of Louisiana's 1,577 Katrina-related deaths.

The wind, rain, and flood stifled virtually all communication and triggered a city-wide power outage. With no way to talk to one another and streets impassable because of high water or downed trees and utility poles, local first responders were stymied. As government reports would later determine, the Federal Emergency Management Agency (FEMA) was initially overwhelmed and woefully unprepared to handle such a major calamity. But even local and state government agencies were slow to act because of bureaucracy and their inability to grasp the magnitude of the crisis.

With little help from the government, the survivors were left to fend for themselves.

In New Orleans, the floodwater didn't drain because the city's pumps were disabled by the storm. As temperatures soared over 100 degrees, tens of thousands of victims were trapped for days in their flooded, sweltering homes without food, water, or medicine. Those who were able to reach the Superdome found that conditions in the stadium had deteriorated into chaos. The same was true at the nearby Ernest N. Morial Convention Center complex, where thousands of other hungry, thirsty victims had sought shelter. It took days—and countless deaths—before vital supplies on a large scale finally reached them.

Along the Mississippi and Alabama coasts, houses looked like they had been bombed. Survivors caked in mud from head to toe walked silently in a daze among the ruins, not knowing what to do or where to go. Again, because of a virtual communication blackout and no easy access into or out of the shattered communities, victims were on their own until the arrival of state and federal agencies days later.

However, in the midst of this staggering disaster, an untold number of heroes emerged from all walks of life. Most notably in New Orleans, ordinary citizens—many of them flood victims themselves—revved up their boats or commandeered abandoned craft and began rescuing neighbors. In the demolished coastal towns, survivors used their bare hands to save victims buried in the rubble. And individual first responders who had lost everything carried out daring rescues on their own initiative.

During the initial paralysis of FEMA and other agencies, one branch of the federal government performed heroically and swiftly—the United States Coast Guard. Within hours after Katrina made landfall, Coast Guard helicopter crews began working around the clock, plucking victims off rooftops, delivering supplies to stranded survivors, and medevacking the sick and dying. Of the estimated 60,000 people who needed rescuing from the floodwaters of New Orleans and the wreckage along the Gulf Coast, the Coast Guard saved more than 33,700 people (about 12,500 by helicopter and 21,200 by boat). The Louisiana Department of Wildlife and Fisheries launched dozens of its boats in an operation that was credited with rescuing 21,000.

More than one million people in the Gulf region were displaced by the storm, according to FEMA. Hundreds of thousands of evacuees scattered to other parts of the country and never returned. New Orleans lost more than half its population after Katrina. But by 2015, the city had nearly 400,000 residents, which was 80 percent of its population at the time of the hurricane.

Today, the scars from the storm are still evident—abandoned, moldy structures that had been office buildings; cement pads where houses once stood; weedy, vacant lots that had been front yards; crumbling pilings that had supported bridges and houses. But after years of recovery and rebuilding, life has returned to a thriving new normal for the people of New Orleans and the Gulf Coast, and they continue to mount an ongoing revival of the region.

But no amount of renewal will erase the memories of Hurricane Katrina—the horror, the heartache, and the heroism.

In the following pages of this book, you will read the dramatic accounts of heroes who gave their all to save others: a clever Boy Scout who kept his family from drowning, dedicated Coast Guardsmen who conducted dangerous rescues, a cool-headed police chief who led a group in a watery escape, a gutsy animal lover who saved more than a thousand stranded pets, gritty medical volunteers who worked under appalling conditions to keep patients alive, a stubborn radio personality who risked death to broadcast life-saving information, and brave flood victims-turned-rescuers who overcame unbelievable challenges.

In lengthy personal interviews with the author, these heroes recalled their harrowing Katrina experiences. Some found it difficult and emotional because of the suffering they saw. Others remembered every agonizing moment with vivid clarity, because it never leaves their mind. The stories are written as factual and truthful versions of their recollections, although the dialogue has been re-created in some cases for dramatic effect.

The courageous souls profiled in this book didn't consciously choose to become heroes. They came to the aid of their neighbors because, in their hearts, it was the right thing to do—no matter the personal cost to their own well-being.

As Earl Barthé, Jr., whose story is featured in this book, said, "We just did what had to be done."

"AIN'T NOBODY ELSE GONNA DIE"

Donald Colletti and Jimmy Pitre

URGENT - WEATHER MESSAGE
NATIONAL WEATHER SERVICE NEW ORLEANS LA
1011 AM CDT SUN AUG 28 2005

. . . DEVASTATING DAMAGE EXPECTED . . .

HURRICANE KATRINA . . . A MOST POWERFUL
HURRICANE WITH UNPRECEDENTED STRENGTH . . .
RIVALING THE INTENSITY OF HURRICANE CAMILLE
OF 1969.

MOST OF THE AREA WILL BE UNINHABITABLE FOR
WEEKS . . . PERHAPS LONGER. AT LEAST ONE HALF OF
WELL CONSTRUCTED HOMES WILL HAVE ROOF AND
WALL FAILURE. ALL GABLED ROOFS WILL FAIL . . .
LEAVING THOSE HOMES SEVERELY DAMAGED OR
DESTROYED.

THE MAJORITY OF INDUSTRIAL BUILDINGS WILL BECOME NON FUNCTIONAL. PARTIAL TO COMPLETE WALL AND ROOF FAILURE IS EXPECTED. ALL WOOD FRAMED LOW RISING APARTMENT BUILDINGS WILL BE DESTROYED. CONCRETE BLOCK LOW RISE APARTMENTS WILL SUSTAIN MAJOR DAMAGE . . . INCLUDING SOME WALL AND ROOF FAILURE.

HIGH RISE OFFICE AND APARTMENT BUILDINGS WILL SWAY DANGEROUSLY . . . A FEW TO THE POINT OF TOTAL COLLAPSE. ALL WINDOWS WILL BLOW OUT.

AIRBORNE DEBRIS WILL BE WIDESPREAD . . . AND MAY INCLUDE HEAVY ITEMS SUCH AS HOUSEHOLD APPLIANCES AND EVEN LIGHT VEHICLES. SPORT UTILITY VEHICLES AND LIGHT TRUCKS WILL BE MOVED. THE BLOWN DEBRIS WILL CREATE ADDITIONAL DESTRUCTION. PERSONS . . . PETS . . . AND LIVESTOCK EXPOSED TO THE WINDS WILL FACE CERTAIN DEATH IF STRUCK.

POWER OUTAGES WILL LAST FOR WEEKS . . . AS MOST POWER POLES WILL BE DOWN AND TRANSFORMERS DESTROYED. WATER SHORTAGES WILL MAKE HUMAN SUFFERING INCREDIBLE BY MODERN STANDARDS . . .

Despite the dire warning from the National Weather Service, 46-year-old Donald Colletti chose to stay in his home. Sure, he knew how dangerous hurricanes were. Having been born and raised in St. Bernard Parish, he had been through several of them—and Katrina worried him. As it bore down on New Orleans and the Gulf Coast, he sent his wife, Rita, and adult children, Donald, Jr., and Natasha, to Texas, telling them he'd join them later. But it was a lie he had to tell. He had no intention of leaving, deciding to remain behind to protect his house and outboard-motor repair business from possible looters after the storm.

On Sunday, the day before Katrina arrived, Colletti took his 22-foot fishing boat, the *Big Fish*, out of the marina, put it on his trailer, and towed it home. On the way, he filled it with 110 gallons of gas and also put fuel in six five-gallon jugs. Then he parked the trailered boat in his front yard.

Longtime friend Jimmy Pitre, 47, who lived across the street with his ailing 77-year-old mother, Joyce McGuire, hollered to Colletti, "We're stayin' back! If this area gets flooded, come get us, okay?"

"You got it, Jimmy," Colletti replied.

That night, as the winds howled and the rain hammered the New Orleans area, Colletti kept receiving frantic calls from family members, begging him to leave. But by now it was too late. Not that it mattered, because he was determined to ride out the storm at home.

Later, as gusts topped 130 miles an hour, he could hear trees crashing and flying debris banging against his groaning one-story brick house. With a flashlight, he ventured outside and was nearly blown over by the fierce winds that were ripping shingles off the roof. *Uh-oh, I screwed up*, he thought. *I should have left when I had the chance.*

Back inside, Colletti noticed water dripping from the ceiling, down the walls, and onto the floor. He grabbed tarps and draped them over the sofa and other furniture. His animal heads—trophies from his hunting trips—were getting soaked in his game room. He took plastic totes that held his hunting gear and emptied them. Then he hurried around the house, snatching cherished family pictures off the walls and collecting his wedding album and his kids' photo albums. He stuffed all the pictures into the totes and put them on the kitchen table.

Through it all, the family pet, a dachshund named Peanut, trembled and stuck close to his master's heels. Colletti tried to get some sleep, but it was impossible, not with the shrieking wind and sounds of blown debris battering houses and vehicles.

The next morning, just as Katrina thundered over St. Bernard Parish, Colletti peered outside. The cascading, wind-whipped rain was pounding the area, while the unrelenting gusts sent fences and parts of roofs skidding down the street, which was covered with a few inches of water.

His fishing buddy Bob Roberts, who earlier had evacuated to a relative's home in Alexandria, Louisiana, about 200 miles northwest of New Orleans, called Colletti's cell phone around 9 A.M. "Brother, where you at?" Roberts asked.

"I'm still home, Bob."

"Man, I've got bad news. The levees broke in St. Bernard. Pretty soon you're gonna be underwater. Get outta there now!"

After the call, Colletti opened the front door. The water on the street looked no worse than it did during any big storm. A short while later, Peanut, who hadn't let his master out of his sight, scampered toward the back of the house. *What the heck is goin' on here?* wondered Colletti after finding Peanut shivering in fear under a bed. Colletti got down on his hands and knees to pull out the terrified dog.

And that's when he noticed the floor was sopping wet. *Water is coming up through the floorboards! That's not from the rain.* By the time he put Peanut into a dog carrier and set it on the kitchen table, water was spurting out of every crack in the molding at the bottom of the walls and under the windows.

Colletti dashed into the living room and looked out the window; he was thunderstruck. Floodwaters had already reached the knob of the front door. Cars and trucks were floating past his house before they had a chance to sink. Caught in a strong 20-mile-an-hour current, the vehicles were bouncing into houses before disappearing from view.

This is unreal! he thought.

Clutching the dog kennel that held his pet, Colletti opened the door to escape to his boat. But the water rushed into the house with such force that it washed him through the living room, dining room, kitchen, and into the game room before he was finally able to regain his footing. During this unexpected water ride, Peanut was dunked several times even though Colletti never let go of the kennel.

He slogged his way to the open front door and waded in the swift current to his boat, which was still attached to the trailer by the bow, causing the stern to bob high. He put his terrified, crated dog into the boat and then went back inside for the totes that contained the photos and, along with some food and other items, tossed them in the *Big Fish*.

The ferocious wind and lashing rain made it difficult to see as he used his knife to cut the rope that was holding the boat to the trailer. Once the craft was freed, gusts pushed it against the house next door and then another.

As soon as he got the engine cranked up, he heard Pitre hollering, "Donald, come get me and my mama!" The flood-waters had risen so high that Pitre and his mother were hanging on to the gutters under the roof of their house.

Battling the wind and current, Colletti steered his boat past floating cars and debris toward the pair. When he finally reached them, he idled the engine. Pitre and Miss Joyce let go of the gutters and gripped the side of the boat. But before Colletti could help them aboard, a savage gust shoved the *Big Fish* across the flooded street to the other side as mother and son desperately held on. The boat became lodged against a house, giving Colletti the chance to grab his neighbors.

"Just let me go," pleaded Miss Joyce, a big-boned woman in ill health.

"Miss Joyce," said Colletti, "one way or another you're gettin' into my boat."

Pitre planted his feet on top of a submerged fence and shoved his mother up while Colletti pulled on her arms to get her on board. Then he helped Pitre out of the water before covering Miss Joyce with life jackets as she lay shivering on the floor of the *Big Fish*.

He gunned the motor, hoping to reach Chalmette High School, a designated shelter about eight blocks away. But six houses down, he heard yelling coming from underneath a neighbor's flooded carport. Three people were trapped in their tied-up boat, which the rising floodwaters had wedged against the ceiling of the carport.

Colletti secured one end of a rope to the *Big Fish* and tied the other end around Pitre, who then leaped into the water and swam over to the jammed boat.

"Jimmy!" his mother rasped. "Be careful!"

"How you doin', Miss Joyce?" Colletti asked.

She nodded, but it was clear to him that she didn't look good. The woman, who suffered from a bad heart, was shaking and extremely pale.

Meanwhile, with some effort, Pitre reached the neighbor's boat. After Colletti secured another rope to his own boat, he tossed the other end to Pitre, who tied it to the stuck craft. The *Big Fish* then pulled it out from under the carport. The three saved people were too afraid to operate their own boat, so Colletti helped them board his.

"When the flood came in, we got out of the house and jumped into our boat," said one of the rescued neighbors. "We couldn't free the boat in time before the water lifted it and trapped us under the carport."

"We're tryin' to make it to Chalmette High," Colletti told them. He turned to look at Pitre's mother and asked, "Miss Joyce, you okay?" She gave him a blank stare, then shuddered and went limp. Colletti kneeled down and felt her pulse but couldn't find one. His heart sank.

Pitre, who was still in the water, let the neighbor's abandoned boat drift away. "Look, Donald!" he shouted, pointing to two bobbing heads in the water. "They're caught in the current. We gotta go get 'em!" Hanging on to the rope that was still attached to the *Big Fish*, Pitre began swimming toward the pair.

"Jimmy!" Colletti yelled. "You need to get in the boat!"

After Pitre returned to the *Big Fish*, Colletti threw his arm around him and said, "Jimmy, your mama is gone. She passed away."

Pitre closed his eyes for a moment and didn't say a word as he tried to process this devastating moment. Finally, he spoke up. "Mama, I know you're gone, but what do you want me to do?" As if he heard her speak, Pitre turned to Colletti and declared, "Donald, ain't nobody else gonna die. We're gonna rescue everybody we can. That's our mission."

"Okay, Jimmy. Let's go get the two in the water."

Colletti maneuvered the boat close enough for Pitre to haul in the pair. Up ahead, a man screaming for help was clinging to a power line that was hanging only a few feet above the rushing water. The force of the current was pushing him so hard that the line was bowed. Just before the *Big Fish* reached him, the man lost his grip and plopped into the water, but Colletti managed to position the boat so Pitre could yank him aboard.

The intense winds and driving rain whipped waves up to 5 feet, making it extremely difficult to steer. As Colletti motored toward the high school, he was flagged by more desperate people who had escaped drowning by scrambling onto their roofs. Others were dangling out of second-floor windows or poking their heads out of holes they had made in their attic.

The blinding rain came from all directions and felt like pinpricks on Colletti's bare skin as he navigated his boat close enough to several rooflines so Pitre could help the survivors hop aboard. Eventually, the *Big Fish*, which was designed to fit six passengers comfortably, was packed with nearly 20 people.

One of those rescued was a little girl, about seven, who screamed when she noticed the dead woman in the boat. "We're all gonna die!" she screeched. "We're all gonna die!" Her hysterics, as well as the waves that were splashing into the overloaded craft, thrust the frightened passengers into wails of doom.

While fighting the brutal gusts, deluge, and rough water, Colletti thought, *These people are gonna kill themselves with fear unless I say something.* "Everyone, shut up!" he shouted. "Let's calm down and pray. Our Father, who art in heaven . . ."

One of the passengers joined in and then another until most everyone was praying. The screaming and crying stopped—except for the girl's. When the passengers finished the Lord's Prayer, they recited it again, but the girl kept howling.

I've got to quiet her, Colletti thought. He summoned her to his side and said, "Little girl, I have a captain's license and I've never sunk a boat. But it's really hard for me to steer it, so I'm gonna need your help. If you see any debris in the water, you let me know so I can go around it. And if it's too hard for me to turn the wheel, I'm gonna ask you to help me, okay?" She nodded and sat next to him—and stopped her bawling.

The crammed *Big Fish* rocked and rolled past several houses where people were perched on the roof, begging to get picked up. "We'll be back!" Colletti shouted to them. "I promise!"

A few blocks from Chalmette High, the boat reached the flooded Judge Perez Drive, a wide four-lane road where, because of its openness, the crosswinds and waves were more dangerous than on the flooded side streets. Several times, the waves almost tipped over the crowded, unstable boat. At one point, when a gust nearly upended the *Big Fish*, Colletti ordered everyone to shift to one side to prevent it from capsizing. After he was able to turn the craft into the wind, he told them to return to their original positions.

When they reached the high school, Colletti motored the boat right into the bed of a submerged pickup truck that was parked on the ramp that led to the gym. Policemen and firefighters who were stationed at the shelter cheered and yelled, "Somebody made it!" The first responders helped the passengers step out of the boat and over the roof of the swamped truck.

"We're so happy to see you," a firefighter told Colletti. "You're the first boatload of survivors to arrive."

"We have a deceased lady in the boat."

"It would cause a panic right now if we take her inside," the firefighter said, referring to the reaction of the people who had spent the night there. "Besides, I don't know where we'd put her."

"I guess I'll keep her in the boat while Jimmy and I go back out to rescue more people."

A deputy came over and gruffly informed Colletti, "It's too dangerous out there. The boat's gonna sink and y'all gonna drown, so I can't let y'all go."

Colletti and Pitre looked at each other and shook their heads in response to the deputy. "There are people clingin' to roofs and light poles and tree branches," Colletti told him. "More people are gonna die if we don't go out there right now."

Pitre chimed in, "We made promises to people that we'd come back for 'em, and we're gonna do it."

Colletti told Pitre, "Push off, Jimmy. We're goin'."

The deputy said, "I ain't gonna be responsible if y'all die."

"Fine with us," said Colletti. "We don't expect you to be."

The two rescuers returned to their drowned neighborhood where they quickly filled the *Big Fish* with more survivors and brought them back to the high school. Colletti asked a firefighter, "Is there anything you can do for Miss Joyce? Her body is freakin' out the passengers."

"Yes, we now have a place for her," the firefighter said. "We'll put her in a classroom."

As they removed Miss Joyce, Colletti took Pitre to the back of the boat, put his arm around him, and made him look away. In as respectful a manner as possible, six firefighters picked up the body and carried it to the classroom. Then Pitre went in to spend time alone with her, while a white-haired survivor took his place for a few rescue missions with Colletti.

When Pitre returned to the boat, the hurricane was still creating havoc, spawning tornadoes and waterspouts, including one that spun toward the *Big Fish*. A 10-foot-long chunk of marshland plummeted from the angry sky and whacked into the side of the boat, spewing mud and grass. About 20 yards away, the waterspout dropped a hot tub on the water. To the men's amazement, a bottle of Soft Scrub remained standing upright on the bobbing tub for several seconds before it slipped off as the tub sank.

While piloting the boat, Colletti had to dodge floating objects like 55-gallon drums, vehicles, and even the trailer of an 18-wheeler. Adding to this unreal world, flames caused by breaks in gas mains were shooting out of the water.

Colletti was guiding the *Big Fish* over a canal that paralleled Chalona Drive when Pitre hollered, "Donald, you're outta the canal!"

"No, I'm not," Colletti replied.

"Well, there's a house in front of us!" It was one of several homes that the floodwaters had lifted off their foundations and shoved across the canal and into an apartment building.

Undeterred, the men continued rescuing people. During one run, the *Big Fish* was packed with more than two dozen victims. Among them were a couple with three children who had been trapped on their roof. After being ferried to Chalmette High, the man of the family gave Colletti a bear hug and said, "Dude, I'm a grown man. But I was helpless. You two saved me and my family. If you hadn't shown up, I doubt we would've survived."

Hearing that heartfelt praise was enough to keep Colletti and Pitre going through the rest of the day. After the hurricane cleared the area, more private boats—including one operated by Colletti's cousin Ricky Colletti—motored up and down the flooded streets, rescuing survivors. Deep into the night, Colletti and Pitre continued their search for stranded people.

Even though the pair had no flashlights, Colletti maneuvered the *Big Fish* between houses, relying on the boat's running lights and the moonlight. They cruised neighborhood streets with the engine idling so they could better hear shouts for help from people confined inside their attics.

Exhausted after making repeated rescue trips, the pair took a break around midnight. Colletti parked the boat on the roof of his house and handed Pitre a sandwich he had made before the flood. "It's only peanut butter, Jimmy."

Pitre, who, like Colletti, hadn't eaten all day, took a bite and replied, "It tastes like steak to me."

They tried to get some sleep on the roof. But they could still hear, from somewhere in the distance, the muffled cries for help and the sharp reports of gunfire and firecrackers from desperate people trying to gain the attention of rescuers.

"Jimmy," Colletti said, "I can't sleep. Can you?"

"No," Pitre replied. "I keep thinkin' about the people out there."

So the pair stepped back in the boat, hoping to trace the cries for help. In some cases, they were lucky and found survivors in the blackness.

The next day turned sunny and stiflingly hot with no breeze. Because of the dead calm, it was easier to maneuver the *Big Fish*. Colletti and Pitre took first responders to several abandoned boats that had been floating aimlessly in the floodwaters. Even though none had keys, Colletti, a boat mechanic since his teenage days, knew how to hot-wire the vessels and got them started so that the first responders could search for survivors.

When the pair delivered that day's first group of victims to Chalmette High, the gym was packed with hundreds of weary, ragged people, some in only their underwear, shorts, or pajamas.

"I don't know what we can do to feed all these people," a firefighter told Colletti. "We've broken into the food store across the street and took as much as we could, but it's still not enough."

"I know what to do," Colletti said. "We'll be back in a little while."

The *Big Fish* motored to a nearby flooded grocery store, which had its front windows blown out by the storm. Colletti backed the boat up to the opening and had Pitre tie off the corners of the stern. Then Colletti gunned the engine. As the prop wash churned the water, it pushed lightweight packaged food like bags of potato chips, snacks, candy, and bread out of the store. The items floated toward the boat, where the men scooped up the edible loot in fish nets and took it all to the school.

Sometimes the pair waded into other flooded grocery or convenience stores to collect canned and packaged foods and bottled water that were sitting dry on high shelves. After delivering the supplies, the men kept a few cans for themselves. Although they were hungry, they didn't consume much. Colletti got tired of eating cold clam chowder out of a can.

On their food runs, the pair was still finding survivors who had knocked out attic vents or cut their way to the roof with chainsaws, hatchets, machetes, and axes. By the third day, helicopters were delivering food and medical supplies that the men took to various shelters.

Whether they were helping to rescue people or gathering food, Colletti and Pitre had to walk, swim, and wade in the disgusting, contaminated water. And that made life miserable for them.

On Friday, the fourth day after the storm, the two borrowed a smaller boat from a neighbor and went to the courthouse to collect supplies for Chalmette High. As they were carting the supplies to the boat, they discovered too late that they were wading waist-deep in an oil slick. When they boarded the boat, they were dripping with oil, making the floor extremely slick. Colletti slipped and fell hard, tearing several ligaments in his knee, chipping a bone in his elbow, gashing his arm and legs, and spraining his ankle.

Making matters worse, his eyes and skin began burning from the oil. He ripped off his clothes, reached for liquid soap and a bottle of water, and quickly washed himself. He and Pitre left the loaded boat unattended and went back to the courthouse where Colletti was given a brace for his knee and a bandage for his injured arm. Because he spent so much time in the foul water, his skin began peeling off in sheets, even between the toes. The same was true for Pitre.

Despite the pain, heat, and hunger, the two fatigued men chose to continue their mission—only to discover that someone had stolen the borrowed boat. So they hopped into another boat piloted by Colletti's cousin Ricky and searched for the thief.

It didn't take long to find him. A few blocks away, they heard blasts from a shotgun. Moments later, they saw the stolen boat turn the corner and head toward them. It was being driven by a lone man with a shotgun. Ricky pulled his boat alongside the thief's and began a friendly conversation. Hiding an aluminum bat behind his back, Colletti jumped into the stolen vessel, saw the shotgun and empty shell casings on the floor, and raised his bat.

The thief was so startled that he stumbled backward. "Don't hit me," he squealed. "I didn't steal nothin'." His hand flopped over the side and into the water and was sliced wide open on a submerged stop sign. He grimaced and then tried to grab the shotgun, but Colletti snatched it first and tossed it overboard. The thief then leaped into the water.

Realizing the thief's hand was bleeding badly, Colletti put the bat down, leaned over the side, and said, "Here's the deal. We're not gonna hurt you. Your hand is cut real bad, so you need to get out of this nasty water right now or else it'll get infected."

They brought him into the boat and treated his wound by pouring alcohol over it and then bandaging it. He was left at a shelter.

Colletti and Pitre were rescuing fewer people with each passing day because more boaters and first responders were helping evacuate stranded residents. The pair was sleep-deprived and beyond exhaustion. During a break, they took stock of what they had accomplished over the previous days. The two figured they had rescued more than 200 people—and that made them proud and want to continue. "Other than my mama, nobody has died on our watch," touted Pitre.

But because they were working in horrible, unsanitary conditions, the men felt mounting stress and discomfort. Even Peanut, who stayed mostly in his kennel on the boat throughout the long ordeal, remained traumatized. He didn't eat or drink for days. During a break, Colletti took Peanut out of his kennel to play with him, but the dog didn't move. Colletti kept talking to him in the same happy tone he always used when he came home from work. Finally, after 15 minutes, Peanut snapped out of his mental paralysis and began wagging his tail, and soon eagerly ate and drank his first meal since the hurricane.

By the end of the week, Colletti was in agony from his arm and leg injuries. His cuts were infected (as were Pitre's) and his right ankle had swollen so badly that he had to cut his boot to get it off. He also was suffering from a painful ear infection.

But what hurt most was the heartache he felt for his family. He wasn't worried about their safety because they had evacuated far from the hurricane's wrath. However, he was tormented by the fact they had no way of knowing whether he was dead or alive. And he couldn't contact them because he had lost his cell phone—which contained the numbers of all his friends and family—when the floodwaters rushed into his house the first day. The thought that they had no idea of his fate gnawed at him day and night.

And then it dawned on him. His newlywed daughter, Natasha Guerra, drove a Yukon that had OnStar, a mobile feature that connected to a live operator. *I can call OnStar, and they can get in touch with Natasha,* he thought. Colletti borrowed a satellite phone from a friend, Jason Licciardi, and reached an OnStar operator. The operator then contacted Natasha, who was driving with her mother, Rita, in Texas and crying because Natasha's wedding song, "It's Your Love," was playing on the radio. The operator broke in and said, "Natasha Guerra? This is OnStar. Your father is alive and well and wants to speak with you."

But Colletti was so choked up with emotion that he couldn't talk. He handed the phone over to Licciardi, who assured Natasha and Rita that Colletti was okay, although he was bruised and beat. Relieved that his family knew he was safe, Colletti felt a heavy burden lift.

Pitre, too, felt tremendous relief after borrowing a police phone to contact his wife, who had evacuated to Tupelo, Mississippi.

"Now I can relax," Colletti told Pitre. In reality, Colletti needed immediate medical care. An officer who was aware of all the work that he and Pitre had done to save lives asked Colletti, "Are you ready to leave the area now?"

"Yes, I'm ready," Colletti replied wearily. "There's nothing more I can do."

Unable to rebuild his house in St. Bernard Parish, Colletti and Rita moved to Poplarville, Mississippi, where he operates A-1 Outboard Motors.

Pitre also left his longtime neighborhood and moved to Lafourche Parish.

Colletti says Hurricane Katrina hasn't changed him much, except in one small way. "I was never scared of weather. But now, if the wind picks up and we get some bad gusts, like from a thunderstorm, I get the heebie-jeebies.

"Otherwise I'm happy every day that I live and breathe. I don't think much about Katrina. But when I do, I know that I have left a legacy to my children and grandchildren that I did something good for other people."

"WILL I BE HOISTING MY OWN NEIGHBORS?"

Coast Guard Helicopter Pilot Craig O'Brien

As Lieutenant Craig O'Brien stared out the windshield of his United States Coast Guard HH-65 helicopter, it was almost too hard for him to comprehend the scene below. The city where the pilot lived and worked was drowning. Thousands of houses were underwater, and thousands more were battered and bashed. Landmarks of the adopted city he treasured had been flooded or destroyed.

Wherever he looked, he saw victims perched on the peaks of roofs, huddled on tops of apartment buildings, and slogging through the oil-slicked stew of fouled water. All were waiting, hoping, praying to be rescued.

And many were being saved, because the Coast Guard was the first federal agency deployed in the hours immediately after Katrina had barreled into the region. Now, like bees hovering over flowers, bright orange-and-white USCG helicopters were everywhere, pulling up survivors from flooded homes and buildings to safety in the largest air rescue in American history.

Seeing the widespread devastation for the first time, O'Brien braced himself for what lay ahead. Sharing his thoughts with members of his crew, he said, "This is the worst-case scenario, and that means it's going to be a long mission. We have a lot of work to do. The task at hand is not insurmountable, but it's going to be extremely hard. This next week will test us in every way possible—our training, our skills, and our mental toughness. We'll probably be doing things we've never done before, but our goal is to save lives and that's what we're going to do."

This was not so much a search-and-rescue mission as it was just a rescue mission, because the crew didn't need to search for survivors. They were everywhere you looked, tens of thousands of them, stranded and shell-shocked.

Some of them were trapped on roofs and balconies in his swamped neighborhood of Uptown. As O'Brien flew over once-familiar streets that were now submerged, his gaze zeroed in on one specific house—his own. Just as he expected and feared, it was engulfed by the floodwaters.

Based at Air Station New Orleans, O'Brien, 32, had lived with his wife, Jana, and their rescue dog, Hudson, in a quaint old cottage near Tulane University. The couple loved the city—especially its food, music, and charm—ever since they settled there two years earlier.

On Saturday, the day before the storm's outer bands arrived, base commander Captain Bruce Jones ordered an evacuation of the station. Its five helicopters were flown to safer areas with crews who planned to return immediately after the hurricane passed. Like other Coasties and their families, O'Brien and Jana scrambled to board up their house. They also gathered important papers and documents to take with them.

At around 10 P.M., they bowed their heads in the living room and said a little prayer for the city and for the people of New Orleans. After bidding a teary good-bye to their home, the couple, with Hudson, drove through the night to a hotel in Lake Charles, Louisiana, about 200 miles west of the city, far from the projected path of the hurricane. Too wired to get much sleep, the couple watched the storm's progress on television.

During one broadcast, a news anchor reported, "The US Coast Guard closed ports and waterways along the Gulf Coast today as Hurricane Katrina nears its expected landfall Monday morning. The Guard said that extensive damage along the coast should be expected. The Guard has moved forty aircraft and thirty boats and cutters in positions surrounding the expected strike zone, and is poised to conduct search-and-rescue and humanitarian missions at the earliest opportunity." (The Coast Guard would ultimately deploy 86 aircraft and 160 boats.)

Late Monday morning, as Katrina moved out, O'Brien received word that the levees had breached. He rushed to the temporary command post in Alexandria, Louisiana, to help coordinate the arrival of all available aircraft and air crews to Air Station New Orleans, which sustained serious damage but was still functional. He also arranged for the Coast Guard to fill a semi tractor-trailer with food, water, and other supplies that had been bought at a local Walmart for delivery to shelters in the afflicted area.

Because he was a decorated, skilled helicopter pilot, O'Brien was needed more in the air than on the ground. Five months earlier, he and three other crewmen had been awarded the Naval Helicopter Association's Aircrew of the Year award for the region. They were cited for "superior airmanship" and "exceptional on-scene management" in the dramatic rescue of the captain of a capsized fishing vessel off the Louisiana coast in poor visibility, high winds, and with the helicopter short on fuel.

O'Brien sensed that what he was about to face in the aftermath of Katrina would be much more challenging than anything he had ever done. At 4 A.M. Tuesday, he woke up Jana and said, "I'm going back to New Orleans. It's real bad. You won't see me for a few weeks."

Later that day, he was in the cockpit of a helicopter loaded with bottles of water and packaged meals ready to eat (MREs). His first landing was on an overpass surrounded by floodwaters and crowded with desperate survivors. When the aircraft touched down, O'Brien winced at the sight. Drawn, weary people—some wearing barely any clothes and others still in disbelief—surged toward the aircraft. Nearby, victims were wading in filthy 4-foot-deep water to reach the dry overpass. All wanted to be rescued immediately. But the HH-65 could carry only about six survivors at a time—maybe a few more depending on the collective weight of the passengers—to a shelter. Just the neediest of the needy were given priority.

It was during another flight on his first day in the air that O'Brien flew over his flooded neighborhood in Uptown. Pointing to a specific roof, he told copilot Kevin Crecy, "That's my house . . . or what my house used to be." It was sitting in at least 4 feet of water.

Is our neighborhood destroyed for good? O'Brien wondered. *How many of my friends didn't leave the city? Is everyone alive down there? Will I be hoisting my own neighbors?*

He recalled a few days earlier urging his good friend and neighbor Brian O'Reilly to evacuate his wife and four children. O'Reilly had given O'Brien a hard time about him and Jana leaving on Saturday. O'Brien had jokingly countered, "Don't have me hovering above your house picking up your family, because I'll be real mad at you. In fact, Brian, if I hoist them off your roof, I'm leaving you behind." But now O'Brien wondered, *Will I be picking them up for real? Are they okay?*

While chaos was the norm on the ground, disorder was the norm in the skies. Within days after Katrina struck, the Coast Guard helicopters plus another 100 choppers from all other branches of the military, the media, and private businesses buzzed over the city without any centralized air-traffic control or coordinated communication.

Adding to the danger, O'Brien and the other pilots had to maneuver in tight spaces while looking out for power lines, cell towers, trees, buildings, and one another. Helicopters were often hovering within several feet of one another picking people up.

As if that wasn't hazardous enough, O'Brien flew at night—he volunteered for that duty—from sunset until the wee hours of the morning. To see better at night, he and his men used night-vision goggles (NVGs). Because most of New Orleans was without power, the city was pitch-black. The only lights visible to the crew were lanterns, flashlights, candles, flares, and even cigarette lighters held aloft by survivors signaling for help. It broke O'Brien's heart to see so many tiny lights, knowing that each one represented a person, a family, or a large group of stranded victims waiting to be rescued.

Normally, a coast guard crew consisted of a pilot, copilot, flight mechanic (the person responsible for the hoists and guiding the pilots into position), and the rescue swimmer (the person lowered on a cable as long as 200 feet to save people). The first night of flying, O'Brien took off without a rescue swimmer because none were available.

Over Uptown, he spotted 15 people stuck on second-floor balconies on a deeply flooded street. Even though it would be tricky to extract them without a rescue swimmer, O'Brien felt confident that the shorthanded crew could pull it off.

Focused on avoiding power lines and the building next door, O'Brien hovered his aircraft while hanging on to every word from flight mechanic Kevin Devault, who was conning (guiding) him into position. Because O'Brien could see only what was in front of him and not what was behind him, he had to rely on Devault.

"Forward and right ten," Devault directed him. "Forward and right five . . . Slow your advance . . . Hold your position . . . Position is good . . . Maintain position."

Amid fallen trees, broken limbs, snapped power poles, and tall bushes that obstructed much of the balconies, the flight mechanic lowered the rescue basket and expertly threaded it down with pinpoint accuracy. There was no sense shouting instructions to the people below, because the noisy helicopter made it impossible for them to hear Devault. Leaning out the open door, he used hand signals to get the survivors—one or two at a time—into the basket, which he then hoisted up. Even though each lift was incredibly difficult, the three-man crew rescued everyone on the block.

Each helicopter flight started with full loads of water and MREs that were distributed to survivors after a landing or an airdrop. As the weight of the cargo grew lighter, the crew was able to pick up more survivors. The flight mechanic became expert at filling each available space of the helicopter cabin with survivors, which included putting little kids in the cargo area.

Every time the aircraft was packed with people, it made a quick flight to a high and dry collection point where survivors waited (sometimes for days, unfortunately) for transportation to a secure shelter, medical facility, or another city. Among the drop-off spots were the University of New Orleans, the Cloverleaf (where I-10 intersects with Causeway Boulevard), and the Superdome.

As the aircraft commander, O'Brien was responsible for the $10-million helicopter, the successful outcome of every flight, and the safety of his crew and the rescued passengers. Over the week, O'Brien flew mostly with his copilot Kevin Crecy, flight mechanic Matt Lotter, and rescue swimmer Ian McPhillips.

One of O'Brien's biggest challenges was how far to push the aircraft beyond its limits during hoists. On his instrument panel were indicators known as "chicklets," lit bars that change color from green (all systems operating) to yellow (nearing the engines' limitations) to red (stressing the engines beyond normal capabilities). He was staring at red chicklets many times during those risky nights. He knew that if he damaged an engine, the aircraft would be taken out of commission for repairs—and that would translate into fewer rescues.

Every night, O'Brien faced a critical situation of needing more power just as the aircraft was nearing its limit. The first time it happened, several passengers were hunched in the back while the crew tried rescuing one more person. O'Brien thought, *I can't put any more power to the engines. If we have any kind of malfunction right now, I'll need to put it down. If something goes wrong at this moment, what can I do so we all survive?* Peering through his NVGs at the trees, power lines, buildings, and unlit cell towers, he planned where he would land in case of an emergency. *Those survivors were alive when we got them off the rooftops, so it's my responsibility to keep them and my crew alive,* he told himself. *If anything should happen to them on my flight . . .* He tried to shake off that terrible thought, which was his greatest fear. He pushed the engines to their max while the final survivor was brought aboard. Then the pilot safely brought everyone to a drop-off location.

But the fear surfaced again later that night. Packed with victims, the aircraft was making its final approach in the darkness when, suddenly, O'Brien spotted through his NVGs two sets of power lines directly in front of him. At the last possible moment, he applied full power, coaxing the helicopter to leapfrog over the lines. His heart pounding wildly, O'Brien told Crecy, "Man, that was close—too close." Well aware that power lines and aircraft don't get along, O'Brien shuddered at a mental picture of the catastrophe that he had averted. *Everyone on board would have been killed.*

Like all helicopter crews, O'Brien and his men were constantly making emotionally draining, tough choices. Whenever they were faced with saving a group of people, the rescue swimmer had to practice triage—determining who would get on board based on their medical condition. Only those needing urgent care were given priority. The frazzled, the thirsty, the hungry would have to wait for hours, sometimes days, for other flights. The first time it happened, O'Brien thought, *These people are all in this horrible situation and it's like we're playing God. But it's the only way.*

He rarely had a break from making a difficult decision. Typical was the time he had six members of an extended family aboard when McPhillips, the rescue swimmer who was on a rooftop with several more survivors, radioed O'Brien, "Can you take one more? It's the grandmother."

If I do, will I overtorque this aircraft? the pilot wondered. *Will we run out of power? I'm in reserve fuel stage. Do I have enough fuel for another hoist and still get them to the collection point and then us to our air station to refuel?* He told the rescue swimmer, "I can't take any more." O'Brien felt terrible splitting up the family, because he knew how important it was for relatives to remain together during times of crisis. He felt terrible a lot. Sometimes, on his return to pick up the rest of a family, he would learn another helicopter had rescued them. What he wouldn't know was if they had been taken to the same place where he had dropped off the first group of family members.

As the week unfolded, the emotions of the survivors grew raw and often explosive. When planning hoists off an apartment building roof, O'Brien couldn't tell, through his NVGs, the state of mind of the people below. Were they relieved they were getting rescued . . . or were they irate that it had taken so long to reach them? Some rescue swimmers on other helicopters had reported being threatened and even attacked by unruly survivors. But McPhillips was able to defuse any troublemakers and make people understand that the best way to evacuate was to cooperate and follow his instructions.

The crew was aware that night rescues were scary for the survivors—especially children—when they were being hoisted in the rescue basket. It was dark. The helicopter was loud. The person was twirling in an open basket more than 100 feet in the air. O'Brien made sure the crew passed out candy like M&M'S and Jolly Ranchers to kids for a little taste of comfort. On the other hand, many children thought it was fun to get lifted into a helicopter for a ride.

Even over all the operational noise—including voices of crewmembers talking at once in his headset and the engines whining—O'Brien could still hear the emotional responses of the people in the back. Some were incredibly grateful that they had been rescued, and they sobbed with tears of joy while thanking and hugging the flight mechanic and rescue swimmer. Occasionally, O'Brien and Crecy, who were too busy to talk to the survivors, would get a pat on the back or a handshake from a grateful survivor. A simple *thank you* or *we love you* meant much to the crewmen.

Seeing the massive devastation from the air, rescued survivors often burst into tears, shouting things like "That's my city!" "Everything is destroyed!" "Is this for real?" "What am I going to do?" "Where will we live?" "What's going to happen to me?"

At the end of each eight- to ten-hour night shift, O'Brien worked during the day at the air station's operations center, dispatching other aircraft and coordinating the distribution of supplies. Meanwhile, his crewmen were loading and unloading supplies, servicing the aircraft, and carrying out other tasks.

The unrelenting heat and humidity made their jobs tougher. Because of damage to the base, there was limited electricity, no air conditioning, and no running water—which meant no showers. The Coasties wore the same flight suits every day and were lucky if they had a change of underwear. Before MREs became available, food the first few days consisted of PowerBars and Gatorade because the crews took their own emergency hurricane rations and distributed them to survivors. Sleep was an afterthought for O'Brien. He managed to squeeze two or three hours of shut-eye in the late afternoon on an office couch.

Before he stepped into the aircraft every night, O'Brien took a moment for a quick prayer: *I know this is going to be hard and the people of this city need me. Whoever you are, Higher Being, you've got to help me out here, because this is beyond me as an individual.* The pilot wasn't an overly religious person. In fact, until Katrina, he had never prayed before a mission. But this time, he felt the need to pray.

To get into a "battle rhythm," he would discuss that night's mission with his crew. "We're operating on the upper edge of our skill set and the aircraft's performance," he reminded them—not that they needed to be. "Don't make this mission routine. If we get tired toward the end of the night, we must still think of the survivors. It might be a bad day for you, but it's a worse day for them. You might be hungry and weary. But they are hungrier and wearier. Continue to treat them like you always do—with the respect they deserve even if they are hysterical. This is an historic event, and you are living history right now. The Coast Guard has a long record of service to this nation, so let's make this a highlight. These people are our countrymen and they need our help."

On his third night of rescues, O'Brien spotted a light flashing through an upper-floor window of a small flooded church near the Xavier University campus. By this time, most trapped survivors were dehydrated and hungry and growing weak. The pilot circled overhead to assess the situation. He faced multiple hazards—tall buildings, an I-10 overpass, power-line poles, and a cell tower.

"This is a real tough environment," he told his crew. "Can we get McPhillips in there?" After a quick discussion, the crew came up with a game plan. They were all trained in vertical-surface rescues, like saving someone clinging to a seaside cliff, so this situation was fairly similar, only in an urban setting.

McPhillips was lowered to the church and then scaled the side to enter through the window.

Hovering between power lines, a cell tower, and the overpass, O'Brien thought, *I hope this is easier than it looks so we can get on with our rescues.*

McPhillips reported back that the man who had signaled them was the church's elderly caretaker. The man was in bad physical shape because he was a diabetic who had run out of his insulin medication. "He's delusional and doesn't want to leave, because he says he needs to get the church ready for Sunday services," McPhillips told O'Brien. "He's under the impression that the city is okay. He doesn't understand that the water is almost up to the second floor."

Knowing that this rescue would be tricky and time-consuming when so many other people could be helped, O'Brien asked, "Can we leave him food and water and come back later for him?"

"Negative," McPhillips replied. "We can't wait until morning. If we do, he'll die. We need to get him out now."

"My fuel situation is critical," O'Brien said. "Stay with him while I refuel."

When the helicopter returned, the crew hoisted the man out of the church and brought him to safety. McPhillips told the pilot, "I asked him why he chose to stay at the church when he knew the hurricane was coming, and he said, 'I knew God would take care of me.'"

"I guess God sent us here to get him out," O'Brien said.

During another mission, an elderly man who had been picked up from a roof suddenly went into cardiac arrest in the back of the helicopter. McPhillips immediately began giving him CPR. Up front, O'Brien wondered, *Do I take him all the way to the emergency room in Baton Rouge [30 minutes away], where they have the equipment to save him, or take him to an EMT [emergency medical technician] at a collection site [two minutes away]?* O'Brien made his decision: He called ahead to the collection site and had an EMT and ambulance waiting for them. Seconds after the helicopter landed, the stricken man was carried into the ambulance, where he was treated on his way to the hospital.

O'Brien and his crew rescued more than just people. They saved pets, too, knowing that for some survivors, their animals were all they had left in the world. "Pets are part of the family," O'Brien told his men. "If we leave them behind, then that adds more stress to the survivors. Pets can help calm them."

Most of the dogs and cats behaved while being hoisted in the rescue basket with their owners. But one time, a rescue didn't go as planned because of a skittish dog. McPhillips was lowered to pick up a man who had been stranded with his two Chihuahuas on a strip of land surrounded by floodwaters east of New Orleans.

Clutching his pets, the survivor was ready to get hoisted when one of the dogs got spooked by the noise of the helicopter and ran off. The man and the rescue swimmer began searching for him.

O'Brien looked at his fuel gauge and radioed McPhillips, "I'm getting into a critical fuel situation. We have only five minutes left. If you don't have the dog by then, you need to get up here. Otherwise, I'll have to come back for you." No pilot wants to leave a rescue swimmer behind, especially in an isolated area. Unexpectedly, O'Brien lost communication with McPhillips. *Are you kidding me?* the pilot thought. *Is this Chihuahua going to have me hang around and exhaust my fuel?*

Time was just about up when they found the dog. "It's all one hoist," O'Brien told Lotter, the flight mechanic. "We don't have time for any more." The rescue swimmer attached himself and the survivor into a nylon sling known as a strop. Then, with the man holding on to his two dogs, they were lifted into the helicopter, which eventually made it back to the air station just before running out of fuel.

By the end of the week, parts of the city were considered more dangerous than others following reports of looting, robberies, and assaults as well as sporadic gunfire—some aimed at aircraft. Several fellow pilots told O'Brien their helicopters had been shot at.

One night while taking survivors to a collection point, O'Brien saw quick bursts of light coming from a specific spot below him. It was hard to tell the difference between flashes from a gun and those from a flashlight, but he figured it was a signal from a survivor. He made a mental note of the location and planned to return to the scene after he dropped off his passengers. But then police told him they had arrested a man who had been firing at aircraft at the exact moment O'Brien's helicopter flew over him. The man admitted to police he fired his weapon because he was mad that more food hadn't been delivered to him.

Another time, O'Brien received word that several survivors were in dire need of food and water on an overpass east of the city. Around sunset, he and his crew took off to deliver supplies to them. Minutes later, as O'Brien concentrated on the landing, the flight mechanic shouted to him, "They've got weapons pointed at us! Get out of here!"

O'Brien saw that several men had drawn automatic weapons and were aiming them at the aircraft. "Well, this doesn't look good," he told his crew. "They don't seem to be very welcoming." He waved off the landing. After circling overhead, he said, "Forget it. No way we're air dropping supplies to them." The helicopter delivered the food and water to a different group—one expressing gratitude for the supplies.

After working for seven straight days and nights, O'Brien was ordered to take a break. Despite feeling mentally and physically drained, he finally allowed himself a brief moment to consider what he and his crewmen had accomplished: They had rescued more than 140 men, women, and children.

O'Brien and his crew were part of the largest coast guard disaster response in its history, involving the deployment throughout the stricken Gulf Coast of 49 helicopters, 37 fixed-wing aircraft, 29 cutters, 131 smaller boats, and 5,600 active-duty and civilian personnel. At the peak of the rescue operation, USCG helicopters were saving 100 people an hour.

Many Coasties were flood victims themselves. O'Brien was one of 582 coast guardsmen whose homes were severely damaged or destroyed by Katrina.

Less than a month after Katrina hit, O'Brien and his crew were in the same area rescuing victims of Hurricane Rita. The Coast Guard was credited with saving the lives of 67 people.

Months later, O'Brien and his wife, Jana—with the help of Coasties, family, and friends—completed repairs of the couple's flooded house in Uptown. In 2006, he was transferred to Washington, D.C., and from 2010 to 2013, served as operations officer at Air Station Port Angeles, Washington. Eventually promoted to commander, O'Brien was made an advisor and faculty member at the National Intelligence University's Center for Strategic Intelligence Research in Washington, D.C.

"As I look back, I truly do not know how my fellow coast guardsmen and I did it," O'Brien says. "With noteworthy faith and morale, the crew of Air Station New Orleans helped save a city despite our own displaced families and significant personal losses.

"Hurricane Katrina made me a stronger person. It has given me a newfound perspective of what's important in life—health, family, and community. Even though my material losses were significant, they really didn't matter. I had a job to do for our country that was way more important."

"WE'LL HAVE TO SHOOT OUR WAY OUT!"

Police Chief John Dubuisson

As torrents of floodwaters gushed into the library where Police Chief John Dubuisson and a dozen members of his force were holed up, he realized they now faced a sudden life-or-death situation.

The front doors had broken open, allowing the water to pour into the building. He knew there were two scenarios—both bad—that would happen if they remained huddled on counters and desktops and didn't do anything: Water pressure would build up and destroy the small library or the onrushing water would fill up the main room and drown them. *Our only hope is to get the back doors open so the water can flow out*, he thought.

Dubuisson ordered his officers to shoot out the glass doors, but the glass was too strong for the bullets. *There's one more thing I can do*, he told himself. The chief jumped into the swelling water, reached the back doors, and pushed them open. But the powerful current knocked him off his feet and carried him outside, where he was slammed hard against an iron railing. Reeling in pain and unable to breathe because he was underwater, he could hear the anguish in the voices of those in the library. They were screaming and shouting, "Chief! Chief! Oh my God! The chief is gone!"

Two days earlier, Dubuisson felt confident that his town of Pass Christian, Mississippi, would be spared, based on weather forecasts that projected Katrina would strike farther east. He figured the small beachfront community of 7,000 people, who lived on a spit of land a mile wide and six miles long, would get hit with heavy wind and rain, but nothing serious, nothing like Hurricane Camille.

He was 19 in 1969 when Camille—one of the most powerful hurricanes ever to plow into the United States—destroyed most of the town. He and his mother, brother, and sister had evacuated before the killer storm made landfall. When they returned the next day, they discovered their house—and everything they owned—was gone.

Now it was Katrina's turn to threaten Pass Christian. New forecasts warned the storm's projected path was much closer, so Dubuisson sent his wife and 14-year-old son to stay with relatives near the city of Biloxi. Then he and Pass Christian's fire chief, Richard Marvil, ordered residents to evacuate.

For a day and a half prior to the hurricane's arrival, Dubuisson, his officers, Marvil, and his firefighters drove up and down the streets of Pass Christian, warning people to leave immediately. In low-lying areas, the police knocked on doors and asked residents for their identification and names and phone numbers of next of kin to contact in case they were injured or killed during the storm. Most people paid attention and fled. Some didn't, especially those who had gone through Camille and believed that since they had survived that hurricane, they could ride out Katrina, because Katrina couldn't possibly be as dangerous as Camille. Or so they thought.

Early Sunday evening, about 12 hours before landfall, Dubuisson stopped to chat with an old friend, Nelson "Nip" Lang, 76, who was leaving a car at the Pass Christian library's parking lot—the highest ground in town. Lang, who had been the local civil defense director years earlier, said he and his wife Helen, 72, were not evacuating.

Dubuisson drove him home. On the way, the chief offered to take Lang and his wife to a shelter, but the man refused. "I've lived in that old wooden house my whole life, and it's survived every hurricane since it was built more than a century ago," Lang said.

"But what about Helen?" the chief asked. "Wouldn't she be better off in a shelter?"

"No," Lang replied. "She's been sick, and she wants to stay home. Don't worry about us, John. We'll be fine. Katrina won't be that bad."

Later that evening, Dubuisson, with his 12-person skeleton crew, manned the command post at the police station. Watching the movement of the hurricane on TV, he grew increasingly worried that Pass Christian would take a direct hit. Driving rain and screeching wind had intensified as the menacing storm surge rolled in.

At about 2 A.M., he heard on the police radio that six of his officers who were in three squad cars reported they couldn't make it back to the station. "Chief, we've got water everywhere," an officer told him. "We can't get out of here."

"Okay, y'all stay where you are, and we'll come get you."

He and Sergeant Michael Lally headed out the door. When they stepped outside, they were pelted by rain that was coming in sideways. They got into a former army deuce-and-a-half—a high-wheeled, two-and-a-half-ton military cargo truck—and drove over and around fallen trees and through flooded streets. The water was rushing from south to north at a rapid pace. "The storm surge is a lot worse than I ever imagined," Dubuisson said. "It's rising fast. I'm not sure we can even make it to the men."

"Oh, we'll get to them," Lally said with confidence. The truck blasted through the water and finally reached the stranded officers. The chief told them, "Line up your cars directly behind us and stay as close as you can. Our truck will push the water out of the way so you can get back to the station."

The squad cars remained right on the truck's tail as the vehicle plowed through the onrushing surge. But when the mini caravan neared Trinity Church, the water was so deep that it rolled in right behind the truck and swept the cruisers off the road. Within seconds, the cars were bobbing like corks in a stream. *There went my three brand-new cruisers*, Dubuisson thought. The police department had bought them just a few months earlier.

The deuce-and-a-half backed up and rescued the water-logged officers and brought them to the police station. Seeing the storm surge continuing to rise, Dubuisson said, "It's time to get out of here before the whole place goes underwater. We need to move our emergency operations center to the library."

The library, which was located several blocks away, sat on higher ground—more than 20 feet above sea level—and had its windows and doors refitted with glass designed to withstand winds from a Category 3 hurricane like Katrina. The chief and the ten officers who were on duty that night gathered computers and radio equipment and drove the remaining squad cars to the library. Also helping and joining them were dispatcher Gloria Sanders, who brought along her Chihuahua, Paco, and warrants officer Rebecca Ruspoli, who was the wife of assistant police chief Tom Ruspoli.

The wailing wind and slashing rain grew more intense through the night. At daybreak, Dubuisson looked out over Scenic Drive and saw that the water level was even with the road. He told the others, "You see that house across from the library? During Camille, the water got as high as that front porch—and that's where the water is right now, and it's still rising. We'll likely get some water in the library, but I think we'll be all right."

As the water rose, the cars in the library parking lot began floating away in the surge. The strong current carried off police investigator James Stewart's personal car. "Hey," said an officer, "it looks like Stewart is driving his car down Hiern Avenue at about seventy miles an hour." Everyone laughed in a moment of gallows humor that broke the tension. They were still chuckling when the car sank.

"Hey, everyone," an officer shouted. "Come see this rabbit on a post."

Expecting to spot a bunny perched on a fence, the others saw that it wasn't an animal but a car, a Volkswagen Rabbit, that had snagged on a post next to the library. Dubuisson recognized the car. It belonged to his friend Nip Lang, who had left it there for safekeeping.

"Everything is disappearing under the water—houses, cars," someone said.

"Well, city hall is still standing," the chief said. "And we're still here."

Dubuisson eyed the library's big double glass doors on the north and south sides of the building. The water outside was now about 4 feet deep, or halfway up, giving the chief the uncomfortable feeling that they were goldfish in a fish tank. He wondered, *Just how tough are those doors?* Then he had an unsettling thought: *If one of them busts open, this place will fill up in minutes. We'll all drown, unless we have a plan.*

"Listen up, everybody," he said. "If for some reason, the front or back doors give way and water pours in, we need to turn around and shoot the glass out of the opposite doors so the water can rush past us. If that doesn't work, we'll be trapped and drown."

The water was seeping in under the doors, but not badly enough to cause any real worry. By now, other than the deuce-and-a-half, there was only one vehicle, a squad car, left in the south parking lot that had not been swept away. Soon it too began floating. The water shorted out the electrical system, causing the blue lights to come on and the headlights to flash. Unlike the other vehicles that the current had carried past the west side of the library, this particular car was bouncing nose down and tail up in the water, straight toward the building.

Dubuisson and several others were standing by the front doors watching the car float toward them. "Surely it's going to turn and go past the library like all the other cars did," he said. But the cruiser kept coming directly at them.

Seconds later, it smashed into the double doors, knocking them ajar. As if the floodgates of a dam had been opened, water cascaded into the library. Tables, chairs, computers, and books were swept from their normal spots and shoved against the opposite wall on the north side of the main room. Everybody scrambled onto desks and counters to avoid getting carried off and body-slammed against the wall.

From atop a desk, Dubuisson, who regretted leaving his gun in his car, shouted to the other officers, "We'll have to shoot our way out! Start firing at the north doors and side panels before the water builds up inside!"

The officers drew their weapons—.45-caliber pistols—and fired about two dozen rounds into the glass. Whatever concerns the chief had about the toughness of the new doors were quickly laid to rest, because the glass didn't break. Each bullet did nothing but make a small spiderweb the size of a quarter in the glass. The officers looked around at one another in surprise and dismay. "That's some strong glass," someone said. "Now what do we do?"

"Somebody's got to find a way to open those doors," Dubuisson replied. "And I guess that somebody is me."

He jumped into the water and waded over to the north doors. *Before you open them, you've got to have a plan*, he told himself. He knew there was a railing for disabled persons on the back porch. *If you get swept out when you open the doors, grab the rail as you go by. If that doesn't work, there's an oak tree about twenty-five yards past that. You must swim to that tree.*

He had a good grip on the wall and the window next to the double doors to brace himself against the force of water that would gush out once he opened them. He reached over to the doors' push bar and pressed it open. The water from the inside surged through the open doors, creating a current inside that was so powerful it knocked him off his feet and carried him outside.

Dubuisson took a quick breath before being swallowed by the water. Tumbling under the surface, he didn't panic. *If I can just grab on to the handicap railing, I can pull myself up and get my head above water.*

To his good fortune, the current pushed him toward the railing. To his misfortune, the force of the water propelled him so hard against the railing that he thought he broke his hip. He was in excruciating pain, running out of air and pinned underwater. *This isn't good*, he thought. Even though water was flowing over his head, he could clearly hear everybody screaming and hollering inside the building, "Chief! Chief! Oh my God! The chief is gone!"

No, I'm not! Dubuisson told himself. Wincing from the pain in his bruised hip and in his oxygen-starved lungs, he pulled himself up onto the first rung of the railing and held on to the second rung. He stuck his head above the waterline and took in several big breaths.

"I'm okay!" he shouted. "Is everybody all right inside?"

"Yes!" came the reply. "Everyone is safe—so far."

The water was up to his shoulders but soon leveled out lower as the current slowed down. "Everybody needs to get out of the building," the chief said. "It's not safe anymore."

"Where will we go?" someone asked.

"We'll get on the roof over the children's wing," the chief replied. "There's an overhang that will give us some protection from the wind and rain."

The library was L-shaped. The larger, main roof had a 5-foot overhang that covered part of the lower roof of the children's wing, which was perpendicular to the main building. "You'll have to work your way through the doors and then get up on the roof," he told them. "There's still a current, but it's less strong where the children's wing meets the main building."

Officer Anthony Piazza jumped into the water and half waded, half swam through the open doors and found telephone wire stapled to the side of the building. He ripped down the wire and brought it back inside. "We'll form a human chain and use this wire as a rope to hang on to," he told the others.

The current was still forceful as Dubuisson and Piazza helped everyone out of the library. Sanders, the dispatcher, gave the chief her Chihuahua, who was in a pet carrier. Dubuisson put the kennel on his shoulder and assisted Sanders through the open doors, where the current was at its strongest around the library. As they inched their way forward, the current caused the chief to lose his hold on the carrier. It tumbled off his shoulder and into the moving water. He tried to grab it but failed. As Sanders screamed in anguish, the dog and its cage quickly sank from sight.

As heartbreaking as it was to lose Sanders's beloved Chihuahua, Dubuisson stayed focused on making sure everyone lived through this killer storm. They snagged a big round reading table that was floating by and brought it to the corner where the children's wing met the main building. Sergeant Lally then went back inside and retrieved a stepladder.

Placing it on the table, one of the officers climbed onto the roof and then assisted the others. The howling wind and hammering rain made it hard for the survivors to hear one another and left everyone feeling chilly. Dubuisson chose to stay in the water because it was warmer. (That turned out to be a mistake, because the water was polluted with chemicals and poisons that has caused skin problems for him ever since.)

Late that afternoon, after the hurricane moved on and the floodwaters from the surge had receded, the group came down from the roof and walked to St. Paul Catholic School, where they planned to spend the night. The chief had been given the keys to the two-story building before the hurricane struck. When they arrived, they saw the church next door was destroyed and the school had been ravaged by the storm.

The school was directly across the street from the police station but sat on higher ground. Judging from the waterline along the walls, Dubuisson figured the storm surge had covered the first floor of the school, which meant the police station had been completely underwater. *Thank God I made the right decision to leave for the library or we all would've drowned,* he thought.

Shortly before dark, the chief went out onto the roof of the school to survey the damage. The sight shook him to his core. Everywhere he looked, he saw nothing but destruction: houses flattened, cars flipped, trees and utility poles downed. It was as if some giant monster had thrown a temper tantrum and destroyed Pass Christian. *There's hardly anything left.*

Several off-duty police officers and firefighters showed up at the school and were relieved that the group was still alive. "We were headed to the police station thinking we were going to recover thirteen bodies," a firefighter told Dubuisson.

Even though the fire station was located on higher ground, it suffered significant flood damage. Four feet of water had flowed into the station, ruining all the fire trucks.

After officials found a vehicle that worked, they drove around the destroyed town and came across their first casualties—an elderly couple who had tried to ride out the storm in their house. When it flooded and collapsed, the man was killed and the woman suffered a broken hip. It took about five hours before first responders from a nearby town could get her to a hospital.

The next day, Dubuisson encountered survivors who were walking around in shock. Entire neighborhoods had been wiped off the map. The only remnants of homes were the cement slabs upon which they once stood. Framed photos, shattered dishware, overturned furniture, and other possessions that represented treasured heirlooms were strewn across the debris-cluttered landscape. Soaked clothes and tattered drapery clung in ghostlike poses on scraps of splintered lumber from smashed homes.

With its lowest point at 4 feet above sea level and the highest point at 30 feet, Pass Christian didn't stand a chance against Katrina's 30-foot storm surge.

When the National Guard showed up, Dubuisson rode around in a LARC, an amphibious military vehicle that looks like a boat on wheels and can plow through wreckage and flooded areas. Surveying the devastation, the chief and town officials were astounded. More than 90 percent of Pass Christian was demolished. It had no running water or workable sewer system. Its natural gas lines were damaged and leaking, creating pop-up fires. Virtually all communications with the outside world had been severed. The streets were nearly impassable, blocked by tons of debris. Sections of the main coastal road, Highway 90, had either buckled or been washed away.

The police department lost not only its station but 12 of its 19 vehicles. Of the force's 18 officers and 4 civilian employees, more than a dozen—including Dubuisson—lost their homes.

Among the chief's first concerns was securing the town from looters. With the help of the Harrison County Sheriff's Office, which lost most of its equipment, the gritty local police officers carried out their duties despite their own personal hardships. In the first days after the hurricane, Dubuisson and his force worked out of a horse trailer, then a larger camper, and eventually a mobile home.

The area had turned into a huge tub of awful-smelling biohazards, including the rotting flesh of dead animals and, from local processing plants, a million pounds each of dead shrimp, processed chickens, and chicken manure. When health teams arrived, they gave booster shots to survivors and first responders.

During search and rescue, the death toll mounted as bodies were being uncovered in the rubble. Dubuisson was surprised to learn that he and fire chief Richard Marvil were supposedly among those killed.

"Everyone thinks we're dead," Marvil told him.

"Why? The last time I checked, we were still alive," Dubuisson cracked.

"I got hold of a satellite phone and called my dad in Florida," Marvil explained. "I said, 'Hey, Daddy.' And he said, 'Who's this?' I said, 'It's Rich.' He said, 'Is this some kind of sick joke? My son is dead. He was killed in Pass Christian during Hurricane Katrina.' I said, 'Darn it, Daddy, it's me, Rich. You don't recognize your own son?' He said, 'Well, if you're my son, tell me where you was born at.' I told him and gave him the name of the street where I grew up in Pennsylvania and he said, 'Well, glory be, you ain't dead after all!' I said, 'That's what I've been trying to tell you. What made you think I was dead?' And he said, 'I heard it on TV. Some cable channel said that the Pass Christian police chief and fire chief were killed by Katrina.'"

"Our deaths were greatly exaggerated," said Dubuisson, who was able to get word to his wife that he was safe. He also learned that she and their son were fine.

On the third night after working long hours with little sleep, Dubuisson climbed onto a fire truck to take a nap on the hose rack. While he was lying there, he thought about the glass on the doors of the library. *They never did break. If the car hadn't hit the front door, we would've stayed in that library and been nice and dry. It's weird the way things work out.*

Then came an intriguing thought: *What happened to the car that knocked open the library doors? Where did it go? It didn't come into the building, even though the water was rushing in. If it* had, it would have jammed up against the other doors, blocking our way out, and we would have died. Somehow, after busting open the doors, the car went around the library. That makes no sense at all. I guess it was just one of those miracles.

Twenty-eight people lost their lives in Pass Christian from Hurricane Katrina. Among the dead were Nip Lang and his wife, Helen. Their bodies were found several weeks after the storm under a mound of debris near their completely leveled home.

Chief Dubuisson says that in a sense Hurricane Camille killed more townspeople in 2005 than it did in 1969, because survivors of Camille, like the Langs, were lulled into a false sense of security that kept them in harm's way during Katrina, ultimately leading to their deaths.

The police department worked out of a mobile home for five years, dealing with a local crime rate that doubled since the hurricane even though the town's population had shrunk by more than half. Many of the crimes were related to thefts of items from damaged homes and new construction sites. Helping the small police force on a volunteer, short-term basis were law enforcement officers from Kansas, West Virginia, Virginia, and Florida.

In 2010, a new $5-million state-of-the-art public safety complex opened in Pass Christian on one of the highest spots in the town. The 12,000-square-foot building is designed to withstand strong hurricane winds.

Dubuisson lost most everything in the storm, which caused major damage to his house and washed it off its foundation. He and his family managed to salvage a small percentage of their possessions. During the year it took to completely rebuild the house, he and his wife stayed in a condominium in nearby Diamondhead while their son attended eighth grade in Jennings, Louisiana, where the boy lived with grandparents.

"There has been a lot of progress in Pass Christian since Katrina," Dubuisson says. "But we're far, far from where we were. It's been more than forty years since Camille, and there are still scars from that storm. With Katrina, it will take eighty to one hundred years to get this place back to normal."

He says that if another hurricane bears down on his town, he will have every member of the police department evacuate. "I wouldn't put my people back in that situation again, and I wouldn't advise any resident to stay. Property is not worth losing your life over. You can build another house and you can buy another car.

"Until you experience what it's like to face a situation where you might die, you can't fully appreciate how valuable life is. Well, I know thirteen people who can tell you how valuable life is."

"WE'RE NOT LEAVING ANYONE BEHIND"

Michael and Carolyn Gerhold

Surrounded by rising floodwaters and crippled by a power blackout, the Lindy Boggs Medical Center in the Mid-City neighborhood of New Orleans had turned into an island of desperation, desolation, and death.

Life-support equipment no longer worked. Neither did phones, toilets, elevators, or air-conditioning. Tap water was contaminated. Supplies of food and medicine were dwindling. Temperatures above 100 degrees were claiming the lives of the weakest patients. And making conditions inside even more horrific, hundreds of panicky Katrina victims were fleeing their flooded homes and swimming or wading to the overrun hospital for shelter.

Cut off from outside help, the valiant doctors and nurses were struggling to care for their 120 patients while assisting hurricane survivors. Not knowing if or when help would arrive, staff members decided to launch their own rescue operation. The big question for them was: How many patients would die before everyone was evacuated?

*   *   *

Michael Gerhold, director of radiology at Lindy Boggs, and his wife, Carolyn, a longtime registered nurse, had chosen to ride out the storm at the hospital. Even though Carolyn wasn't on call and feared hurricanes, she had volunteered to take another nurse's shift. Trying to ease her mind, Michael said, "The hospital is the safest place you could be. You've got doctors, medicine, generators, food, and a strong building."

The couple arrived at Lindy Boggs on Sunday, bringing with them their cat, Nia, and also big pots of gumbo and jambalaya that Michael had cooked up the day before. Bracing inside the five-story brick building for Katrina's Monday-morning assault were about 300 people, including patients, a small group of doctors and nurses, other employees, and family members of patients and staff. With them in a separate area of the hospital were their pets—45 dogs, 15 cats, and 2 guinea pigs.

The medical staff's major concern was the welfare and comfort of the terminally ill, the transplant patients, and those recovering from surgery or suffering from acute illnesses. A separate hospice facility, which leased space at the hospital, had seven patients who were hovering near death.

Late Sunday night, the Gerholds hunkered down with their cat in an empty patient's room on the top floor as the hurricane's outer bands reached the city. "Okay," Michael told Carolyn, "let's get through this."

The winds grew stronger and ripped off the roof of the elevator shaft, creating a terrible shrieking sound in the shaft that could be heard throughout the hospital. Several windows exploded from violent gusts and flying debris, prompting staffers to move some patients into the hallways.

With their trembling cat, Nia, lying on top of them, the couple went to sleep with hopes that it would all be over by morning. But when Michael woke up shortly after dawn at the height of the storm, he peered out the window and saw Bayou St. John overflowing onto the streets. "Oh, no," he muttered. "This doesn't look good."

The sight brought back memories of 1965 when, as a 15-year-old, he and his parents and sister endured Hurricane Betsy. He remembered how the water rose relentlessly over the street, the sidewalk, the lawn, and up the front steps of the family's raised house in St. Bernard Parish. When floodwaters reached 4 feet inside the home, the family was rescued by a neighbor who had a boat. Hearing people banging from inside their attics and shouting for help, Michael and the others in the boat broke through several rooftops to save them. Later, he and a buddy found a boat and paddled into a flooded grocery store through its broken plate-glass window and loaded up with food and supplies. Then the boys brought them to the second floor of a funeral parlor where rescued elderly people were staying. Although the Lower Ninth Ward and St. Bernard Parish were flooded, most of the city was spared.

But not this time.

"I think we're in for some big trouble," Michael told Carolyn.

As a precaution, the emergency room, which was located on the first floor, was relocated to the recovery room area on the second floor. The kitchen, which had been in the basement, was partially dismantled and brought to a higher floor along with food supplies. Later, the city's power grid failed, so the hospital's generators kicked in to provide electricity to the building. But the floodwaters kept rising until they spilled into the basement, where the main electrical distribution systems were located. The building engineers were forced to shut down the generators, cutting off the hospital's last major source of power.

With no time to spare, the Gerholds and other staffers rushed to move patients to the upper floors. Because Lindy Boggs had no working elevators nor lights, patients had to be helped or carried up the dark, slippery stairwells. It wasn't always easy. Some patients—including a wheelchair-confined 400-pound woman—needed as many as 4 people to haul them up the steps.

Other staffers scrambled to deal with an even more pressing issue. Without power, the electric ventilator machines, which helped the most critically ill patients breathe, stopped working. Dialysis machines designed to keep kidney patients alive also shut down. Carolyn knew that without dialysis, patients would slowly die as poisons built up in their bodies. A small generator on the floor and batteries kept some of the machines going, but they eventually ran out of power. Personnel were unable to use electronic devices for IV medications. Doctors were making rounds by flashlight.

In some cases, nurses like Carolyn used Ambu bags—hand pumps that have to be squeezed to blow oxygen into the lungs of patients who couldn't breathe on their own. Every squeeze is like a new breath. To keep from having their hands cramp up, nurses took turns pressing the bags and even taught patients' relatives to do it.

While carrying out their duties under such difficult conditions, Carolyn and the other nurses tried to maintain a positive attitude in front of the patients. When a patient asked her how soon help would arrive, Carolyn thought, *Not soon enough,* but said, "It shouldn't be too much longer."

But in reality, help was not on the way because of massive confusion, delays, and indecision by government officials in charge of first responders. Besides, no one on the outside knew what awful crisis was unfolding in Lindy Boggs because phone service had been cut off. Some staffers tried to text family and friends for help. But cell service seldom worked, and of those receiving texts from the hospital, many were hoping to get rescued themselves.

Meanwhile, from every direction, desperate neighbors who had been flooded out of their homes were arriving by the dozens. Some paddled in pirogues (pronounced PEE-rowgs), flat-bottom, pointy-ended, canoelike boats popular in Cajun country. Other victims were being towed on air mattresses, inner tubes, and other inflatables by people wading or swimming in the filthy water.

Lindy Boggs administrators told their security guards that

the facility couldn't accept any more people. Michael challenged the officials' decision, claiming, "This isn't a hospital anymore. It's a rescue center now. We have to let everybody in. We can't turn anyone away."

Officials reluctantly agreed, even though the growing number of survivors only worsened the hospital's dilemma.

Among flood victims brought to Lindy Boggs were 96-year-old twins—sisters who had never been separated before—and their niece. X-ray technician Cathy Musso made it her mission to look after them.

Able-bodied survivors and patients' relatives were assigned various tasks. A runner system was set up to relay messages throughout the hospital. Flashlights lit the way along the gloomy hallways, stairways, and patient-care areas.

Without refrigeration, the kitchen staff had to prepare food before it could spoil. The cooks heated up Michael's gumbo and jambalaya over Sterno cans for a few lucky people. But because there weren't enough supplies for the swelling population in the hospital, food was rationed. Dinner for many would eventually be nothing more than grits and bottled water.

On the day of the hurricane, Michael and Carolyn hadn't seen each other until their paths crossed around 4 P.M. "It's getting a little scary," she told him. "When are we getting out of here?"

"I don't know," he replied. "You'd think first responders would be here by now. We're a hospital, and we should be a priority. But, hey, you're fine. I'm fine. We're going to be okay. Let's continue doing what we can to help the patients."

By Tuesday, Lindy Boggs was facing one predicament after another. Because there was no electricity to power the air-conditioning, temperatures in the building climbed to a sticky 104 degrees, a factor that sped up the deaths of several terminally-ill hospice patients.

One floor below, a nurse had written a poignant request on a piece of cardboard: PATIENTS DYING; PLEASE BE RESPECTFUL.

Victims who spent any time in the toxic floodwaters were beginning to show signs of infectious, water-borne diseases. Anyone vomiting or suffering from diarrhea was isolated from the rest of the population. The supply of antibiotics was limited, and everyone was ordered to wash their hands often with anti-bacterial soap.

The massive flood compromised the city's water and sewer systems, so people were told not to drink from sinks or water fountains because of contamination. Toilets couldn't be flushed either to prevent sewer backups. As a result, people in the hospital had to defecate in plastic bags that were placed over the toilets. The bags were then put in larger bags that lined the inside of garbage cans. When the cans were full, the big bags were removed and the cans sanitized. The stench from human waste in the airless, unbearably hot hospital made some people gag.

Because the pharmacy was locked and in the flooded basement, hospital officials worried they would run out of medicine. Michael had an idea, saying, "Where do you get medicine from?

Doctors' offices. Every doctor has free samples. They've got rooms full of them."

The hospital's facilities director, Randy Springer, had keys to the medical building next door that housed many doctor's offices. Given the keys, Laurence Amberson, husband of human resources director Sherry Amberson, and Michael headed out. But reaching the building meant the men would have to wade through the tainted water that was now 5 feet deep.

Clad in a set of scrubs and work boots, Michael didn't want to think about the dangers he was exposing himself to while slogging in the chest-high toxic swill. *Just do what you have to do*, he told himself. *They need the medicine.*

After the men entered the building, they took every sample medicine they could find—antibiotics were the most prized—and filled a few large garbage bags. Michael and Laurence made several trips to and from the building, hoping their finds would help keep patients alive, or at least comfortable. During their trips they also brought back full jugs from water coolers, bottled water, and packaged snacks.

By the time Michael had completed his mission, his arms, legs, and chest felt like they were on fire, because his skin had come in contact with poison chemicals in the water. He stripped off his clothes and bathed under a flashlight in his office, using a washtub filled with a saline solution designed for cleaning wounds.

Like most everyone at Lindy Boggs, the Gerholds were seeing rescue helicopters hoist people from nearby buildings and houses. But none of the aircraft were coming to the aid of the hospital, which now was packed with more than 500 people.

Staffers painted signs on cardboard that said SOS, NEED MEDICINE, WATER, AIRDROP and placed them on the roof. Nothing happened. So they ramped up the message by exaggerating: 30 PEOPLE DIED TODAY, PREDICT 50 FOR TOMORROW. HELP! There was still no response.

That evening, while discussing the hospital's plight, Dr. Glenn Johnson, a cardiologist and vice chief of staff, told his colleagues, "I cannot believe this is happening here in the United States. We're not in Somalia. We're not in Rwanda. I feel betrayed by my government. Well, we can't sit around and wait for a rescue that isn't coming. It's time for us to get everyone out of Lindy Boggs any way we can. It would be a good thing if we had boats."

Michael gazed out the window at the American Can Apartments building a couple of blocks away and said, "I have an idea. All I need is a screwdriver, wire cutters, and a pair of needle-nose pliers."

That night, as he and Carolyn were getting ready to sleep, he told her, "We're going to evacuate everyone tomorrow."

"Oh, really? How?" she asked. "Are we all going to swim out of here?"

"No, we're going to borrow some boats over at American Can. I noticed there were boats on trailers stored on the parking deck."

Early the next morning, he and Laurence took a small aluminum boat and paddled over to the ramp of the apartment complex's outdoor parking deck. Because the electrically powered security gate no longer functioned in the blackout, the men were able to shove it open. They met a security guard, his wife, and two kids, who had been staying in an RV on-site. The guard said he and his family had huddled in the stairwell shaft during the peak of the hurricane.

When Michael explained why he and Laurence were there, the guard was reluctant to let them take any boats. "Look, man, we need the boats to evacuate sick people who will die if we don't get them out of there," Michael explained. "And we have hundreds more people who will end up becoming patients if they aren't evacuated, either."

"Okay, I understand," said the guard. "But I don't have the keys to the boats."

"Not to worry," said Michael. Holding up his tools, he said, "These are my keys. I've rebuilt motors and worked on cars since I was a teenager. I know how to hot-wire a boat."

Michael examined about 20 boats and picked out an 8-foot-wide, 18-foot-long stable, flat boat with a 150 horsepower Yamaha motor. "This is perfect," he declared. "It can go in shallow water and tight quarters and won't tip over." He also chose a similar one for Laurence.

The guard had a pickup with a hitch, so he towed the trailered boats into position and helped launch them off the parking deck ramp. Using his tools, Michael started up the motors.

"Hey," said the guard. "You're not going to leave us here, are you?"

"No," Michael replied. "Y'all can come with us."

The two men piloted the boats right up to the emergency ramp of the hospital with plans of transporting survivors and patients to a dry strip along the levee of Bayou St. John. Coast guard helicopters were buzzing over all sections of the city, rescuing victims. But with no direct communications with the Coast Guard, Michael didn't want to drop off patients and have them stand out in the blazing sun for hours waiting for a helicopter that might not come.

"I have an idea," he told his colleagues. "We'll lure the Coast Guard into picking up our people."

"How?" someone asked. "We've tried to get their attention without any luck."

Michael replied, "I'll show you how to get those helicopters to land."

The first group he took to Bayou St. John were older Lindy Boggs employees dressed in hospital gowns to make them look like patients. On the levee, they started waving at aircraft passing overhead. In no time at all, a Coast Guard helicopter landed and picked them up. On their short flight, they described the hospital's desperate situation and its efforts to evacuate people and patients two boatloads at a time. Before long, two large helicopters directed by an air-traffic controller were transporting the Lindy Boggs evacuees from the bayou landing zone to official drop-off points. Although helicopters couldn't land on the hospital roof, they were able to deliver cases of bottled water, MREs, and nutrition bars.

The two boats were slowly but methodically evacuating dozens of people at a time. To fuel the boats, Michael siphoned gas from doctors' cars into empty five-gallon water jugs through a plastic tube designed for enemas.

Patients who were leaving were given a summary of their medical chart. Around their neck was a pouch with a three-day supply of medications and instructions on how to administer them. Hospital officials planned to evacuate the sickest patients first once a medical facility was located that could handle them. In the meantime, relatives and children, including those of the patients, were among the first to leave.

When officials learned that FEMA had turned the terminal at Louis Armstrong New Orleans International Airport into a temporary medical facility and evacuation staging area, Lindy Boggs' most critical patients were being prepped for the move.

One of them was Carl LaSalle, 32, who had undergone a challenging liver and kidney transplant days earlier. He was lying on a stretcher and being ventilated, because he couldn't breathe on his own. Carolyn noticed that his wife, Jessie, was suffering a cramp in her hand from squeezing the Ambu bag. "Let me take over for a while," Carolyn told her. "We can take turns until we get him into a helicopter."

Also by his side were the couple's four-year-old daughter, Alicia, and Carl's mother. "I'm praying that he's going to make it through this," Jessie said. "I have faith in God that we'll be all right." As he drifted in and out of consciousness, she whispered to him, "I love you."

When her daughter dozed off, Jessie said, "She cries at night. She's upset about her daddy, and the heat and the darkness. I have to rock her to sleep and sing lullabies. I heard her praying, 'God, please protect my daddy.'"

Although family members of patients were urged to evacuate, Jessie declined, saying, "I'm not leaving Carl's side." However, she did send Alicia and Carl's mother on ahead. "We'll join you later," she promised. To Alicia, who was sobbing because she didn't want to leave, Jessie said, "Don't cry. Be brave and keep praying. It'll be all right."

Unexpectedly, members of the Shreveport Fire Department arrived in boats and took command of the evacuation. A fire captain wanted to seize Michael's and Laurence's boats. "No, you're not taking them," Michael said defiantly. "We're doing fine on our own."

Declaring the Lindy Boggs crisis a "mass-casualty incident," the firefighters ordered a field triage of the patients. Doctors were told to grade the patients on their condition: "A" for those who could walk on their own, "B" for those who needed wheelchairs or other assistance, and "C" for those who were critically ill and being ventilated.

When facing such a large-scale calamity, firefighters are trained to rescue as many people as they can as quickly as they can. That means helping the most able patients first, because they are the easiest ones to evacuate. After the majority of the

"A" and "B" patients were rescued, then the firefighters could concentrate on the "C" patients—the most helpless and critical of all—who would take much longer to move. At least, that was the theory.

In gut-wrenching fashion, doctors were forced to decide who would go first and who would be last, even though those at the bottom of the list were the ones closest to death or needing the most care. Each patient was given a tag with a letter on it. When doctors ran out of tags, they used a marker pen to write the assigned letter on the patient's forehead.

Carl LaSalle was labeled a "C" patient, horrifying Jessie. When her pleas to have the firefighters take Carl immediately were denied, she screamed, "How can y'all do this? You're inhumane! You're treating us worse than dogs!"

As cruel as it sounded to evacuate the sickest patients last, the firefighters believed the critically ill were better off waiting at Lindy Boggs where at least they would be cared for until fully equipped medevac helicopters could transport them. Besides, there was no place in the city to take patients other than the temporary setup at the airport, because all the other local hospitals were flooded or overcrowded.

Still, the decision upset many staffers, including Michael. "If you are triaging patients, you take care of the sickest patients first," he said to his colleagues. "All of a sudden, it's just the opposite. Now the worst of the worst get out last."

One patient who was convinced he'd be abandoned went berserk, so nurses had to physically restrain him and strap him to a stretcher. Scolding him, Carolyn said, "You're acting crazy, so stop this right now. You're upsetting the other patients. We'll get you and everyone else out of here soon."

"No, I'll be left behind," the patient claimed. "I know I will."

"My husband is out there driving one of the boats," Carolyn said. "He's not going to leave me behind, so just think about that." After the patient regained control of his emotions, she told him, "I'll untie you if you promise to behave yourself. And, later, when it's time, I'll personally help you onto a boat. How about that?"

He agreed and soon was so composed he began assisting others for evacuation until it was his turn to leave.

Michael continued to ferry people from the hospital, comforting those who were having difficulty dealing with the disaster. He was pleased with the progress of the evacuation, which, by early evening, had airlifted 400 patients, staffers, family members and neighborhood survivors from Lindy Boggs. But then came jarring news.

"Our command post has ordered us to bring an end to the evacuations," a fire captain told Michael. "Too many reports of gunfire and violence throughout the city. Obviously, if we don't take care of our own team, you can't expect us to take care of anybody else. We have to look out for our own safety first."

"And what about the safety of the rest?" Michael growled. "There are at least one hundred fifty people inside, including the most critical patients. What about them?"

"I'm sorry. We were prepared to stay until everyone was out. But now we can't. My commander was able to buy us an extra forty-five minutes. We have to be out of here by sundown."

Michael threw his hands up in dismay. "There's no way we can evacuate everyone in so short a time."

"Do the best you can. Leave the sickest patients behind."

Michael snapped, "We're not leaving anyone behind."

Pressured by the urgency, Michael and his colleagues hustled people into boats at a much faster pace. There was no time to coddle slow-moving patients, no time to coax frightened people, no time to argue who stays and who goes. Rather than wait for patients to step into the boats, staffers carried them on board to speed up the loading process.

While Carolyn was ushering people into the boats, Dr. Johnson told her, "You must be exhausted like the rest of us. Why don't you get in this boat and get out of here?"

"No," she said. "I won't leave my husband behind. I'll go when he goes. And I know he'll be driving the last boat."

When the evacuation finally came to a halt, the fire captain told Michael, "We're not coming back tomorrow. Orders."

Most everyone had been taken out of Lindy Boggs except for 80 staffers, including the Gerholds and family members who volunteered to stay back with the remaining 30 patients. Relatives of the patients were devastated that their loved ones had been left behind, none more so than Jessie LaSalle, who was terrified her husband, Carl, would not be rescued in time.

Knowing of Carl's dire condition, Michael told the nurses, "We're not going to let Carl die when we can do something about it. You keep taking care of him, and we'll get him out of here in the morning."

Then he went over to Jessie and told her, "I don't want you to worry. Tomorrow, we'll carry him down the steps, put him in the boat, and take him to a helicopter. I guarantee you."

She gave him a tearful hug and said, "I believe you."

That night, like the previous nights in Lindy Boggs, neither Carolyn nor Michael slept much in the smelly, broiling building, even though their aching, sweat-drenched bodies cried out for rest. "I'm just too tired to sleep," Carolyn said. "And I feel dirty and gross."

"It's almost over," he said.

The next morning, the hospital staff gently brought each of the remaining patients down the unlit, slick stairway and placed them in the boats. The patients were taken to a nearby patch of dry land where a helicopter pilot had landed and agreed to evacuate them.

When Carl was put in a boat, Jessie told Michael, "I'm so happy to get Carl out of here. Thank you. You're our angel."

Carolyn got in the boat with Carl, who was hooked up to an oxygen tank. After she assisted him into the helicopter, she returned to the hospital and helped load the boats until everyone, except for a few who chose to stay with the pets and the deceased, were evacuated.

When it was the Gerholds' turn to board the helicopter, Michael took a deep breath and said simply, "Thank God, it's done."

Nineteen bodies were recovered from Lindy Boggs Medical Center, including those from the hospice center. The abandoned, damaged hospital never reopened.

After the evacuation, Dr. James Riopelle, an anesthesiologist, remained at Lindy Boggs to care for all the pets that patients' families and staff members had brought to the hospital with them. When word of his dedication to the animals reached the media, Tenet Healthcare, which owned Lindy Boggs, and Oprah Winfrey's production company dispatched two helicopters, which rescued Riopelle and the pets a week after the hurricane struck. The animals were transported to Dallas, where they were placed in foster homes until they were reunited with their owners (like Nia was with the Gerholds).

Carl LaSalle was medevacked to Baylor University Medical Center in Dallas, where he showed rapid improvement until an infection set in. He died on October 7, 2005, five weeks after the Lindy Boggs evacuation. Shortly before his death, the Gerholds visited him and his family at Baylor.

Today, the Gerholds live in Covington, Louisiana, where Carolyn, who's now retired from nursing, tends to her garden and volunteers at Love on a Leash, a nonprofit pet therapy organization. Michael, who continued to work in the radiology field after Katrina, operates a mobile X-ray company.

"WE'RE THE GO-TO GUYS NOW"

Ken Bellau, Earl Barthé, Jr., and the Soul Patrol

They were private citizens who came from different backgrounds, led dissimilar lives, and never met. But they shared a common bond—they loved their hometown of New Orleans and would do anything to help their fellow residents. So when local, state, and federal officials seemed paralyzed in the early chaotic days after Hurricane Katrina, many otherwise ordinary people took charge, in their own separate ways, to rescue thousands of victims.

Among such heroes: Kenny Bellau, who used a "borrowed" fishing boat to lead out-of-town National Guardsmen in daily rescue missions, and Earl Barthé, Jr., who teamed up with his buddies on the "Soul Patrol" to bring hundreds of neighbors to safety.

Ken Bellau, a 37-year-old professional cyclist, was racing in French Guiana in South America when he heard that Katrina was barreling toward his cherished city. Returning home a few days after the hurricane struck, he was relieved his house in Uptown wasn't flooded, although it did sustain roof damage.

His girlfriend, Candy Johnson, who was in New York, had posted on the New Orleans newspaper *Times-Picayune*'s website, NOLA.com, that Bellau was in New Orleans to see if his cat was safe. Within hours, more than 200 evacuees had posted messages asking if he would also check on their pets. Before long, hundreds more people wanted him to find their relatives who had chosen to remain behind.

Although cell-phone service was spotty, Bellau was receiving text messages from Johnson with names and addresses of people and pets. Late in the afternoon on his first day back in the city, he donned borrowed military fatigues and strapped on a .40-mm handgun to give the impression he was with law enforcement or the military.

After Bellau found a pirogue, he spent hours rescuing people trapped by the flood. The unstable boat could carry only two or three persons at a time, so his work was slow. Near a major intersection that was underwater, he paddled to where two dozen motorboats belonging to out-of-state law-enforcement agencies were tied up. Officers told him they were standing pat, because reports of snipers shooting at rescuers made it too dangerous to enter flooded neighborhoods. Frustrated by their inaction, he decided to do what little he could by himself, because lives were at stake.

At one residence, Bellau gathered two cats and a dog and then spotted a man and a woman on the porch of a house that was on fire. He coaxed the woman into his pirogue moments before a fire department helicopter overhead released thousands of gallons of water on the blaze. Unfortunately, much of the water doused the boat, pitching Bellau, the woman, and the cats, into the disgusting floodwater. He got the woman and pets back into the pirogue and brought them to dry land.

While some survivors were happy to see Bellau, others refused to go with him. At one flooded house, a feeble elderly woman stood on her stairway one step above the waterline and told him in no uncertain terms that she was staying. Ignoring his pleas, she said, "Just leave me be, because I have everything I need. Besides, the Lord will take care of me."

Against his better judgment, Bellau left her. When he returned two days later, he found her dead, lying facedown in the water at the bottom of the stairs.

On his second day in the pirogue, Bellau searched for a bigger boat so he could rescue more people. As luck would have it, he waved down a 24-foot sport fishing boat known as a Skeeter. He told the four men on board about the list of people and pets that he was trying to locate. Believing he was a military policeman by the way he was dressed and armed, they let him join them.

The leader of the group was a minister who explained they were from a halfway house for recovering drug abusers. They had gone into the parking garage of a medical building next to Baptist Hospital and taken the Skeeter, a new boat with a quiet, top-of-the line Yamaha F250 outboard motor and state-of-the-art electronics. They also took a ski boat after hot-wiring the ignitions of both to start them.

The men used the boats to help evacuate staff and patients from the flooded hospital and then began rescuing people in the nearby water-logged neighborhood. The Skeeter was taking survivors to a prearranged location, where the water depth was less than 3 feet, to meet a man who drove a heavy-duty pickup. After the evacuees transferred to the truck, the driver would transport them to dry land. Every hour, he would return to the same spot and wait for the Skeeter to arrive with another load of victims.

After Bellau hopped aboard the Skeeter, it took only twenty minutes to cram it with more than two dozen people. During one of the short boat trips, Bellau and his fellow rescuers helped a large family of four generations—from an infant to a 95-year-old man—out of their flooded home. Then the Skeeter motored over to a swamped Louisiana National Guard truck that was dead in the water. The passengers in the boat made room for the ten Guardsmen who had been stranded in their truck. The Skeeter was so overloaded that it listed from one side to the other as water constantly lapped over the gunwales (the upper edge of the boat's sides).

The Skeeter was usually filled way beyond capacity. Whenever Bellau and his fellow rescuers pulled up to an apartment complex, they tried to take everyone at the same time, because there was no guarantee the boat would return. The rescuers knew that at any moment they could be mistaken for looters and arrested, get shot at by snipers, or have the police or bad guys commandeer their boat. And there was also the concern that the Skeeter could break down or sink after hitting something underwater.

Several times a day, the boat's propeller banged into a submerged car, truck, fence, or other object or got caught in downed power lines. Whenever the prop was snagged, one of the men had to jump into the water to unravel it.

By the end of Bellau's first day on the Skeeter, about 150 people had been rescued. The next morning, when Bellau met up with the men, the minister handed him a screwdriver and said, "Here's how you start the boat. I'm taking my guys out of here, because they aren't doing well. They've been at this for several days, and they're exhausted. It's your boat now. Be careful."

So Bellau took the Skeeter out by himself and soon felt extremely vulnerable. Twice, people pulled guns on him, and twice he was shot at. He was constantly on guard for those who wanted to take over the boat. Despite the dangers, he continued his lone rescue mission.

Some survivors were afraid to leave their home, because they knew it would be looted once they left. Bellau understood their worry, but he had a more difficult time comprehending the anger displayed by several victims who lashed out at him because it had taken so long to be rescued. Although he knew they were stressed and hurting emotionally, he took their condemnations personally. However, wrath was far outweighed by gratitude from survivors who hugged and kissed him.

Constantly on edge, Bellau coasted down the flooded streets, listening and looking for victims—while keeping a wary eye out for bad guys. He was drenched in sweat from the blazing sun and suffocating humidity.

Whenever he broke into a house to check on a person or pet, he rifled through the pantry to get food and water for himself and survivors. While inside, he also searched for rope and string or ripped electrical cords off of lamps to use as makeshift leashes for the animals that he rescued.

Midway through his second day alone on the Skeeter, Bellau was mentally drained. Taking a break, he lay down in the boat and decided to beach it, walk away, get into his car, and leave. But then, in the eerie quiet—broken only by the constant whir of helicopters overhead—he heard young voices yelling "Help!" in unison. He cruised for several minutes until he found the source—people of different ages in a house surrounded by water.

After everyone was aboard, a woman gave Bellau a thank-you embrace. When she looked in his eyes, she sensed he was troubled, so she began comforting him even though she had lost most everything. At the meeting point where the pickup truck was waiting, the driver asked Bellau, "So, I'll see you here in an hour?"

"No, this is my last trip," Bellau replied. "I'm done. I'm out of here."

Overhearing the conversation, the woman grabbed Bellau's arm and said, "It doesn't matter that you're white and the people needing help are black. These are your people. You can't leave them out there. You're the only one in the neighborhood who's rescuing them."

Her powerful words shook him up. Needing time to collect his thoughts, he piloted the boat down flooded Napoleon Avenue and pushed the throttle wide open. As the Skeeter rooster-tailed at 45 miles per hour, it zoomed past a speed limit sign that was poking out of the water. It read 35, which made him laugh.

Reaching much shallower water on Claiborne Avenue, he stopped to pick up a stranded father and teenage son. Unexpectedly, two military Humvees roared toward him from opposite directions and trapped the boat. While soldiers in the vehicles trained their guns on Bellau, one of them said, "Our commanding officer wants to speak with you."

Convinced he was being arrested on suspicion of looting, Bellau tied up the boat and went with the soldiers. He was taken to Sophie B. Wright Charter School, which wasn't flooded and now housed a unit from the Second Battalion of the 185th Armor National Guard from San Diego, California. After learning Bellau was a native New Orleanian who knew the city, the officer said, "Do you mind sticking around and helping us? We'd like you to assist in water rescues."

Whatever doubts Bellau had or misgivings he felt about further rescues had left him. *This is what I am supposed to be doing*, he thought.

Every morning for the next two weeks, Bellau showed up at the school. Accompanied by several soldiers, he took the Skeeter out in search of abandoned boats for rescuers to use. They always needed new craft, because most boats lasted only a day or two in the harsh environment. The Skeeter, however, always started and ran all day, every day.

With a couple of soldiers assisting him on the Skeeter, Bellau worked off the list of names that Candy Johnson had texted him. Along the way, they rescued many victims not on the list.

To better hear shouts for help, he turned off the engine and glided down side streets or propelled the boat with a pole. He sounded the boat horn and hollered, "Anybody there?" Block after block, people emerged from windows and attics and boarded the boat. Those who didn't want to leave were given water.

At the end of each day, Bellau and the soldiers returned to the school where they stripped down and had a hazmat team spray and scrub them with antibacterial solution. He and the soldiers would then receive new fatigues. Every evening, Bellau hid the Skeeter and covered it with branches or a tarp and used the pirogue to reach his car on dry land. More than once the Skeeter was stolen and had to be retrieved after a search of the neighborhood.

One morning, a New Orleans police officer joined Bellau and the soldiers for a few hours aboard the Skeeter. During the rescue of a family, the officer pointed to a ski boat two blocks away and told Bellau, "Those guys are looters." The ski boat turned off a side street and disappeared.

Later in the day, Bellau was piloting the Skeeter when he spotted the looters' ski boat, which had a bicycle sitting in the bow. A National Guard officer who was with Bellau ordered, "Let's go get them."

Bellau followed the ski boat's wake, which led them to a house where the boat was docked. Two men were standing on the porch, acting like nothing was wrong. Bellau maneuvered the Skeeter so it pinned the ski boat against the porch. A search of the suspects revealed they had guns, and more than $11,000 in cash, jewelry, and watches. The suspects were turned over to the police.

By the end of the second week, Bellau had helped bring hundreds of people to safety in 92 official water rescues. His work was done. For that matter, so was the Skeeter's. It was banged up from bow to stern, and its propeller had been ground down to a nub from all the objects it had struck. Because a major water pumping station in the city was working again, the flood level had dropped, leaving the Skeeter high and dry near the intersection of Napoleon and Claiborne. Other battered, abandoned pleasure boats were beached nearby.

On his last day assisting the National Guard, Bellau showed a military chaplain the boat. Someone had draped a small, faded American flag over the gunwale. Scattered on the dirty floor were empty water bottles and smelly trash as well as toys and mementos that survivors had brought with them but left on board, including a framed high school diploma.

Two women walked over to the Skeeter, and one of them said loudly enough for Bellau and the chaplain to hear, "It looks like there was a party going on here. It's a shame people were out joyriding when they could have been doing some good."

The chaplain strode over to her, and said, "You don't know what you're talking about." Pointing to Bellau, he said, "That man used this very boat to do some good. He rescued hundreds of people with it."

The woman offered a terse apology and left. But her comments upset Bellau, who by this time was emotionally worn out. *People need to know what the Skeeter did*, he thought. With a marker pen, he put his phone number on the side of the hull after first writing: THIS BOAT RESCUED OVER 400 PEOPLE—THANK YOU!—KEN BELLAU.

When the parents of Earl Barthé (pronounced bar-THAY), Jr. decided to evacuate on Saturday, two days before Katrina's expected landfall, his father, Earl Sr., asked him, "Are you ready to go?"

"I'm not goin' nowhere," Earl replied.

"But Mama packed a bag for you."

"I'm stayin'. I gotta be ready to clear downed trees, and I want first dibs when people need their houses repaired."

Everyone in the Seventh Ward neighborhood knew Earl "Golf Shoes" Barthé, Jr. He was the man with the beard and the colorfully knitted Rasta beanie; the Good Samaritan with a heart of gold; the professional caddie, bricklayer, carpenter, furniture mover, handyman, and jack of all trades. And Barthé knew everyone, too, having lived on the same block since the day he was born 45 years earlier. There was no way he was leaving the neighborhood, not when he felt his people would soon need him big-time.

"I'm prepared," he assured his father. "I've got canned food, water, batteries, flashlights, fuel oil, and gas lanterns."

Earl Sr. knew better than to argue with his strong-willed son. So did several friends who, before evacuating, called him crazy for remaining behind.

After boarding up his house and helping relatives do the same to their residences on the street, Barthé assisted neighbors who were leaving ahead of the storm.

Promising to look after a friend's van and car, Barthé parked the van Sunday night in his driveway. Dog-tired from a full day's work, he sat in the van and said a little prayer: "Thy will, Lord, will be done, not mine. Give me courage and strength to endure what you will for me." He closed his eyes and fell asleep.

Barthé woke up the next morning to shrieking wind and torrential rain pounding the sides of the van. He turned on the radio and learned that Katrina had made landfall 60 miles south of New Orleans and was heading his way. He calmly ate a can of fruit cocktail as he watched debris flying by and shingles blowing off roofs.

A while later, he moved his friend's car to a grassy median that was higher than the street level. As he gazed out the windshield, he saw a white line, about two blocks away, moving from house to house toward the vehicle. *I've lived here 45 years, and I ain't never seen nothin' like this,* he thought. *This ain't normal.* Then it dawned on him. *Lord, is that water comin' in?* He wasn't aware that the city's levees were starting to fail.

Barthé ran over to the van and jumped in. The street quickly turned into a river, about 18 inches deep and rising. Water trickled into the van and reached his ankles. "Well, Lord, what are we supposed to do now?" he said out loud. Seconds later, a wind-battered, solid wooden fence across the street took off like a rocket and slammed into the van. He watched transfixed as the fence flipped, sailed up, and smashed into the redbrick house next door. Then he looked back. Behind where the fence once stood was a flat-bottom boat. "Lord, you brought me a pirogue!"

He hopped out of the van and waded in the fierce storm to the boat. Just then he heard two neighbors on the corner yelling, "Golf Shoes! Golf Shoes! Help us! Help us!" A slender man was carrying a much larger woman on his back through waist-high water.

Barthé paddled the pirogue over to the couple, jumped out, and helped the woman into the boat. Then he and the man walked it back to the neighbor's house. "This is the safest place for you to be," he told them. "There's water in the house, but I don't expect it to rise too much higher. Stay inside until the winds die down."

"What about you, Golf Shoes?" the man asked.

"I gotta see who else needs my help."

Barthé jumped into the pirogue and, while battling the wind and rain and avoiding downed trees, picked up a neighbor who wanted to check on the condition of his food store a few blocks away. On their way to the store, more water rushed into the neighborhood as other sections of the levees collapsed.

Seeing a boy trying to cross the flooded street, Barthé feared the current would pull the child under, so he hollered, "Stay where you at!" He tried to reach the boy, but the powerful gusts and current shoved the pirogue into a telephone pole so hard that the impact put a crack in the boat.

Barthé squinted in the driving rain but lost sight of the child. Then he saw the boy's arm stick out of the water briefly before disappearing for good. Barthé tried but failed to find the boy. "We just lost one," he told his passenger, the store owner. "How many more will we lose?" Heartsick over the drowning, Barthé said, "What more could I have done? It's so hard to control the boat, 'cause the winds are too strong."

After dropping off the store owner, Barthé swapped the pirogue for a bigger flat-bottom boat that he found. As the winds slowly diminished, he paddled around the neighborhood, ferrying survivors to higher ground.

That evening, he stopped at the home of a neighbor and friend James Bijou, known in the neighborhood as "Uncle

Jimmy," who was getting ready to feed a nephew and two of the young man's pals. Unfazed by the storm or the flood because his house was sturdy and on higher ground, Uncle Jimmy was making smothered pork chops with rice and gravy on a gas stove illuminated by a flashlight, since power had been knocked out throughout the city.

The aroma of home cooking reminded Barthé how famished he was. So when Uncle Jimmy gave him a plate of food, Barthé began devouring it, prompting the host to caution, "Hey, Earl, slow down. It ain't goin' nowhere."

Feeling better with every lip-smacking bite, Barthé began tapping his foot on the floor of the darkened front room. Strangely, with each tap, he heard a slight splashing noise. *What's that all about?* he wondered. He pointed a flashlight at his shoes and saw water coming up between the floorboards. "Oh, oh, I think we've got a levee breach," he told the others. "Heads up, boys. This could get real bad. We need to get to the attic."

Barthé and Uncle Jimmy hustled throughout the house, putting certain valuables and heirlooms up as high as they could. Uncle Jimmy found his niece's wedding dress in a box and placed it on top of a bunk bed.

Once that task was completed, Barthé noticed there was one pork chop left, so he sat down and ate it as if he didn't have a care in the world. He acted calm since the others were unnerved by the rising water. When he polished off the pork chop, he joined everyone in the attic and soon fell asleep.

At the first light of day, Barthé hopped into his boat to see the extent of the flooding. It was much worse than he imagined. People were huddled on rooftops or leaning out second-floor windows of flooded houses, begging for help.

He soon met up with lifelong friends Jadell Beard and brothers Ricky and Manny Mathieu, who had a 15-foot flat-bottom boat and a motor boat known as a chopper. They swapped accounts of how their residences, like Barthé's, were flooded.

"I'm in the house tryin' to pick up my furniture," Ricky told the others. "My three-year-old granddaughter Rikailah says, 'Papa, the water is comin' up.' The water was at my ankle and within twenty minutes it was at my knee. I think, 'We're in trouble.' I throw a life jacket on her and put her on the dinin' room table. Then I grab as much stuff as I can. I go outside and the water is up to my neck, and the wind is blowin' sixty miles an hour. I get my aluminum boat and tie it to the railin' by the side of the house. I put my granddaughter in there along with her dog, Wedo.

"Another guy in the neighborhood is bobbin' in the water. I get him in the boat and tell him to look after Rikailah, and then I go help Manny. We spent a couple of hours tryin' to get his boat out 'cause of the wind and all the obstacles."

Beard said that when the water started flowing into his house, he waded outside. "I thought about this little handi-capped girl who lived down the street, and then I saw her mama on the porch," he related. "I went over to them, and when I did, the wind got hold of my raincoat and blew it up like a balloon. I used an air mattress and helped the mama and brought her across the street and then I brought her little girl and their dog. Who knows how many others are trapped in their homes just like they were?"

After hearing their stories, Barthé told them, "We can't wait around because we don't know if any help will ever arrive. It's up to us. We're the go-to guys now."

Bringing Wedo, a white pit bull with black eyes, as their mascot, the men headed out in their boats and began filling them with Katrina victims.

Among the first to be rescued was a multigenerational family of 14 who were perched on their roof. Barthé and his buddies helped them into the boats and brought them to St. Augustine High School, which had been turned into an emergency shelter. Never in his entire life did Barthé imagine that the school—his and his father's alma mater—would one day be a sanctuary for victims of the city's flood of the century. When that became full, the men transported survivors to McDonogh 42 Elementary School, and then to a ramp off I-610, which became a temporary drop-off point.

Hour after hour, day after day, Barthé and his pals rescued people and pets from their swamped death traps—babies, gang members, children, elderly, and those who were pregnant, mentally disabled, or wheelchair-bound. The disaster was an equal-opportunity troublemaker.

Time and again, Barthé had to calmly persuade survivors who were petrified of water to board the boat. He comforted them, put life jackets on them, and let them know that everything would be all right.

At one flooded house, he carried out an elderly woman in his arms. When her feet touched the water, she screamed in terror. "I got you, Mama, I got you," he said reassuringly.

She wasn't convinced and pleaded, "Well, hold me tighter!"

During the evacuation of a flooded residence damaged by fallen trees, victims needed to climb over a railing. Barthé, Beard, and Manny lifted a bedridden man out of the house, over the railing, and into the flat-bottom boat. But two young women, who each weighed about 300 pounds, were afraid to leave. After much coaxing, one of them made it to the railing and then said, "I can't climb over it."

"Look, sister, if you don't, you're gonna die here," Barthé warned. "I'm gonna help you." He bent over in the water until he was under her rear end and pushed her up and over the railing. When she stepped onto the front of the boat, her weight jacked the stern out of the water. The men had to reposition the passengers to keep the boat from capsizing before Beard helped the second young woman in the same manner.

At another flooded house, a woman in her twenties stood in the water on her front porch and said she wouldn't leave, because she was waiting for her father who had left during the height of the storm to summon help. Seeing something suspicious, Ricky rowed around to the backyard and found the father's body floating in the water.

Knowing the woman was mentally fragile and unable to care for herself, Ricky and Barthé decided to lie. "Your daddy left in a helicopter," Ricky told her. "He's waitin' for you at the drop-off. Come on, get in the boat with us." After some reluctance, she did.

The men dealt with children who refused to come out of their homes, because they were afraid of seeing bodies floating past them. To keep the little ones from being traumatized, whenever the men saw a drifting body, they tied it to a tree or utility pole.

After a boatload of survivors was unloaded at St. Augustine, a woman pleaded with Barthé to take her to her family across town. He refused, saying, "There are people in the water and on rooftops who need us now. I can't waste time takin' you someplace else. You're safe here."

"But I gotta get to my family," she insisted. "I'll give you three hundred dollars."

"Your money don't mean nothin' to me," he snapped. "You can't buy me to take you any more than you can buy your way to the gates of heaven."

Often Barthé had to jump in the water and, with a rope, pull the boat around or over fallen trees, utility poles, and submerged vehicles. One time, he swam to a house where the flood had reached halfway up the first floor. To gain entry, he went underwater, wedged himself between the porch iron railing and the front door, and kicked in the door. But while he was under, he accidentally swallowed a bit of the toxic water. He came up spitting whatever was left in his mouth, but the contamination had already entered his body. He suffered diarrhea for three days.

At night, Barthé and his fellow rescuers camped out on the rock-and-tar-paper flat roof of the flooded rectory of the Church of the Epiphany, where earlier they had rescued a priest and a nun. Calling their little settlement Camp Epiphany, the men had quilts, blankets, a large American flag, and a propane-fueled barbecue grill, so they enjoyed hot meals at night. If victims were hungry, the rescuers brought them to the camp and fed them. Other survivors gave the men food, water, and fuel to share with others.

Barthé's cousin, Edwin Barthé, was a skilled mechanic who kept the boats and motors, which took a beating, in working order. "With wire, a screwdriver, and pliers, you can make anything run," marveled Barthé. Edwin was also an excellent cook, and he and Beard kept the bellies of rescuers and survivors full.

After not seeing a single trained first responder for two days, the men met a group of firefighters who gave them three hundred pounds of food and two Jet Skis. "You keep doing what you're doing, Earl," said a fire captain.

Four days after the flood, Barthé and his fellow rescuers came across a boat carrying several game wardens from Lafayette, Louisiana, who were staring at a map. "That map ain't gonna do you no good when all the streets are under-water," Barthé told them. "What're y'all doin' here?"

"We're here to help rescue people" came the answer.

The wardens joined Barthé and his fellow rescuers in getting survivors out of their houses and to the drop-off point. At the end of the day, the wardens were fed gumbo at the camp and then guided by boat out of the neighborhood.

"Hey, what do they call you?" a warden asked.

Ricky replied, "Just call us the Soul Patrol." Then he sped off. The nickname was in honor of legendary rock guitarist Jimi Hendrix, whose song, "Power of Soul," carries the refrain, "With the power of soul, anything is possible." To the members of the Soul Patrol, anything *was* possible—and they were proving it every day.

They began spray-painting *SP* (for Soul Patrol) on houses to let authorities know that the group had rescued everyone inside. Countless residences throughout the Seventh Ward sported the letters *SP*.

Lying on the roof one night, exhausted as usual after another long day, Barthé was struck by a moment of deep reflection. He told his fellow rescuers, "Have you noticed a spirit that has come upon us? Nothin' compares to the energy in ourselves that's allowed us to rescue people day in and day out. I never felt like this before." Looking up at the starry sky, he prayed, "Lord, may the spirit descend upon us every day and remain with us forever. I don't ever want to be without it."

Sleep was not easy for the Soul Patrol. Every time they closed their eyes, they saw visions of suffering victims and heard cries for help echoing in their head. "It rings in my ears night after night," Barthé confided to his friends, "like a ghost whisperin' to me."

After ten grueling days of saving an estimated 500 lives, the men were advised by New Orleans Police Chief Eddie Compass, who was Barthé's friend since high school, to end their homegrown rescue operation because they were increasing their risk of severe health problems. But by then, most of the residents of the Seventh Ward had already been brought to safety by the Soul Patrol.

After their final trip, Barthé shook hands with his fellow saviors and said proudly, "When it was do or die, we did."

The Skeeter that Ken Bellau used to rescue 400 people was turned into an improvised neighborhood shrine. People put flowers and notes of appreciation in the boat as it lay by the side of the road for months until a salvage company hauled it away.

Because his name and phone were written on the hull, the owners of the boat—New Orleans residents Ward Howard, Jeff Haynes, and Dr. Terry Habig—contacted Bellau and invited him to a cookout, which he accepted. At first, he was afraid they wanted to sue him for wrecking their new boat, which had logged only twenty hours on five fishing trips before the storm. But the owners just wanted to hear his story about their boat's role in saving lives. (Besides, the boat was fully insured.)

"Without the Skeeter, I'm not sure how things might have been," Bellau told them. "She was like a good friend, like a beacon of light."

The story made the news. "We were thrilled to have found the boat, but especially happy to find out it was used for such a good purpose," Haynes told reporters later. Added Howard, "For it to have been as useful and dependable as it was, we all think that's great. The boat is banged up now, but she couldn't have died a nobler death."

Bellau was so deeply affected by his Katrina experiences that he suffered depression and post-traumatic stress disorder for several years, which led to his breakup with his girlfriend, Candy Johnson. Eventually, he worked his way out of his emotional state and got back together with her.

The Skeeter's legacy lives on. The Louisiana State Museum found the boat in a salvage yard in 2010 and made it the centerpiece of a new permanent exhibit, Living with Hurricanes: Katrina and Beyond, at the museum's famed Presbytere on Jackson Square in the French Quarter of New Orleans. Bellau gave a moving speech at the exhibit's opening.

Later, he proposed to Johnson in front of the Skeeter in the Presbytere. She said yes, and in 2014, they stood in the exact same spot and exchanged their wedding vows.

Today, Bellau is the head coach of the Tulane University Cycling Association and is writing a book about his Katrina experiences called The King of Uptown. He said the theme of the book is "good people will prevail when times are bad."

*   *   *

The members of the Soul Patrol helped rebuild their own homes and those of others, and today live in the same neighborhood that was ravaged by the hurricane.

Earl Barthé, Jr., established the Soul Patrol Restoration Foundation, a nonprofit organization that mentors troubled youths and seeks to turn them into productive members of society.

In 2010, Barthé, Ricky and Manny Mathieu, and Jadell Beard, along with local residents Steven Mathieu, Dwight Boudreaux, and Thomas Peters, were honored by the New Orleans City Council for their actions in rescuing hundreds of victims. "These citizens put their lives on the line to save others during a dangerous and uncertain time," said Councilman Jon Johnson. "This kind of selfless bravery should be honored and remembered. We are so grateful to have these upstanding gentlemen call New Orleans home."

Said Ricky Mathieu, "There was no option for us. The government wasn't there. Nobody else was there. We had to step up."

Added Beard, "God gave me the strength and helped me do things I didn't know I could do. Seeing the look in the eyes of people when we brought them to safety was worth it."

Recalling all that the Soul Patrol had accomplished, Barthé says today, "We had no idea where we were going throughout this whole ordeal. But we wound up being where we were supposed to be."

"IT'S TIME TO SAVE SOME LIVES"

Coast Guard Rescue Swimmer Laurence Nettles

Mayday! Mayday! Please help us! I'm with my daughter and her premature baby in a boat! Mayday! Mayday!"

The woman's fear-laced voice was nearly drowned out by the clamor of other distress calls heard by coast guard rescue swimmer Laurence "Noodles" Nettles and his fellow crewmen while flying over the Mississippi River Delta directly behind the tail of Hurricane Katrina. The crew's HH-65B Dolphin helicopter was being buffeted by fierce 65-knot winds and blasted by heavy rain, but none of that mattered. The Coasties were determined to find and save the women and the baby in what would become the first air rescue of the killer storm.

The day before Katrina was forecast to make landfall, the New Orleans–based crew of coast guard helicopter 6514— flight commander David Johnston, copilot Craig Murray, flight mechanic Warren Labeth, and Nettles—flew to Lake Charles, Louisiana, 200 miles west of the city, to safety. Their chopper was one of five from Air Station New Orleans that had been moved out of harm's way. The plan called for them to return as early as possible after the storm left to begin rescues.

Nettles, 27, stretched his 6-foot, 190-pound frame on a cot and tried to get some sleep in the crew's temporary quarters to prepare for what he figured would be a busy day ahead. That was what he lived for—to save lives. Being a coast guard rescue swimmer was the perfect job for the physically fit, energetic six-year veteran, who loved challenges and doing crazy things. He was a trained medic, survival technician, and your best friend when you needed an air-sea rescue.

As the storm came ashore early the next morning in lower Plaquemines Parish, about 60 miles south of New Orleans, winds were peaking at more than 125 miles an hour, pushing water over the levees. In the hamlet of Nairn, a few miles from where the center of the storm made landfall, Bobbie Jean Moreau, 58, her daughter Tasha Cheramie, 22, and Tasha's 4-month-old daughter, Cassidy, were trapped in their 129-year-old house. Water from the storm surge soon neared the second floor, where they huddled with their three small dogs.

Cradling her granddaughter, Moreau was wracked with guilt for not evacuating earlier when she had the chance. Now she feared they would all die. The heat in her bedroom was suffocating, causing Cassidy and Tasha to fall ill. Moreau prayed as she fanned her grandbaby, a preemie who weighed only three pounds when she was born several weeks ahead of the due date.

The water kept rising and was now halfway up Moreau's bed. Realizing that they faced certain death if they remained in the room, she told her daughter, "We need to get on the roof." She tore the canopy that hung over her bed and fashioned a rope by twisting and knotting it. "We'll use this to help steady us onto the roof." Then she used a belt to fashion a makeshift life jacket for the infant.

By the time they exited through the window onto the porch roof, the wind had died. Moreau assumed the storm had passed, but she was wrong. In reality, the eye of the hurricane—which is always calm—had moved over the area. She failed to realize that raging winds and pelting rain would soon begin hammering them from the other direction.

After the hurricane made landfall, Nettles and his fellow crewmen, along with those in the other four coast guard helicopters, headed to Houma, Louisiana, 50 miles southwest of New Orleans, to prepare for rescues. As they neared Houma, winds were gusting above 60 knots, forcing the choppers to land hard and shelter behind a tree line. When the winds eased as the eye of the hurricane approached, the Coasties took on fuel and unloaded unnecessary equipment to make room for survivors.

Clad in a shorty—a bright orange short-sleeved wet suit that extends to the knees—Nettles checked his gear, including life vest, helmet, and radio. He was poised for whatever life-and-death situations might arise.

*   *   *

After making it safely onto the roof with their pets, Moreau and Tasha were horrified at what floated past them in the floodwaters—debris from wrecked homes, snakes, a dead horse, a human body. Spotting a neighbor's tied-up boat, Tasha jumped into the water and swam over to it. The 24-foot aluminum boat had a small cabin in the bow and was powered by two outboard engines. Tasha started it up and drove it to the side of the roof of her mother's house. Then Moreau handed the baby to her daughter, passed down the three dogs, and hopped in.

Rain began coming down in torrents and the wind picked up. Moreau and Tasha crouched in the little cabin, shielding Cassidy from the elements. Even though Tasha had gunned the engines, they were no match for the powerful gusts that were pushing the boat toward the Mississippi River. Suddenly, flying debris crashed into the cabin, breaking the window and forcing the women to duck behind the dashboard.

Unable to battle the wind, they let the boat drift until it was caught in the branches of a submerged tree. Because the boat was snagged but not secured, it nearly capsized twice from several strong gusts. When the storm surge leveled off, the women freed the boat and tried to motor back to the house. But the strong winds and current wouldn't let them reach it, so they wedged the boat under a clump of downed trees about 100 yards away.

Despite the ugly weather, the Coast Guard helicopters lifted off at Houma and fanned out in search of anyone who needed rescuing. The flight plan for Nettles's chopper 6514 called for it to head south toward the mouth of the Mississippi River and then turn north and follow the backside of the storm. He, like his fellow crewmen, listened for any distress calls. But because they were flying over the sparsely populated southwestern section of the delta, there was hardly any radio chatter.

The helicopter followed the river, which was the only recognizable geographical surface feature, because so much of the delta was underwater. Awed by the vastness of the flood, Nettles thought, *Any moment now we're going to start hearing distress calls.*

Fearing for their lives, Moreau and Tasha prayed and sang hymns. In desperation, Moreau turned on the boat's radio and began pleading for help. She went from one channel to the next, yelling, "Mayday! Mayday!"

Not hearing any replies, Moreau worried that she, Tasha, and Cassidy were the only survivors in lower Plaquemines Parish; that everyone foolish enough to have stayed behind had died. It was either that, she thought, or the radio didn't work. She fired one of the boat's two flares, hoping it would alert someone to their position. There was no response.

Moreau tuned the radio to the next channel, 16, and again shouted, "Mayday!" She didn't know that channel 16 was the marine distress, safety, and calling frequency.

Suddenly, Moreau and Tasha heard a man's voice. "I'm in a boat near the Empire Lock," he said. "It's where I've been riding out the storm." He was about seven miles south of the women. "It's terrible here. Everything is gone. Everything is underwater."

"Can you help us, please?" Moreau implored.

"I can't," he replied. "But stay on this channel. The Coast Guard monitors it."

After he clicked off, Moreau kept hollering, "Mayday! Somebody help us. Can you hear us? Can you hear us? Mayday! Mayday! Please help us! I'm with my daughter and her premature baby in a boat! Mayday! Mayday!"

Helicopter 6514 was about 25 miles from the small fishing village of Port Sulphur when the crewmen's headphones sprang to life with distress calls. Survivors were yelling and screaming over one another, making it difficult for Nettles to understand what they were saying. No matter the voice, one word kept coming through: *Mayday!*

But in the noise of the radio traffic, Nettles and the rest of the crew also clearly heard two other words: *premature baby.*

"This is the United States Coast Guard," David Johnston, the flight commander, radioed back. Hoping other survivors on the channel would remain quiet, he said, "To the woman with the premature baby, what is your location?"

"Nairn!" Moreau responded, bursting into tears. "Just south of Port Sulphur. We're in a boat by a tree close to the house with a blue metal roof. Hurry!"

It's time to save some lives, Nettles thought.

"Should I fire the flare gun?" Moreau radioed.

"No," Johnston replied. "Wait until you hear the helicopter. We need to get a better fix on your location." He and copilot Craig Murray kept Moreau talking and even told her to count backward from ten slowly so the helicopter's directional finder could home in on her radio signal.

Nettles could hear the panic in the trembling voice of "the woman with the premature baby"—which was how the crew referred to her over the radio to avoid the confusion with other survivors trying to break into the conversation.

As the helicopter was being bounced around in the turbulence over Nairn, Nettles and the others stared out the windows at the flooded delta below, searching for the boat and the house with the blue metal roof. They knew they were close, but they were having trouble finding it.

"Do you see us?" Johnston radioed to Moreau. "Launch the flare when you see us."

A minute later, Murray shouted to the crew, "I see a flare!" Nettles and the others saw it, too. Then they spotted the boat lodged under the trees. Usually, when rescuing people off a boat, Nettles would be lowered onto the vessel. But, seeing that the trees and downed power lines were in the way, he told himself, *I'm going for a swim.*

Johnston and Murray brought the helicopter into a 100-foot hover. With flight mechanic Warren Labeth working the hoist, Nettles was lowered on a cable. On the way down, he was trying to think of the best way to get the trio out. The moment he hit the water, he disconnected himself from the hoist cable and swam to the boat.

Climbing aboard, Nettles said what he often said to victims in similar situations: "Hey, how are you guys doing? Need a ride out of here?" It was his way of trying to calm them. After giving each woman a reassuring hug, he stared at their drawn faces and quivering bodies. He knew they were scared, nervous, and probably in some shock. He then made a quick check of the baby, who was curled up in her mother's arms. *The baby looks okay*, he thought.

"We'll get you all to safety—no worries," he said confidently. "You'll go up in a basket to the helicopter, and then we'll take you to dry land. Everything will go smoothly. We've done this dozens of times and we haven't lost anyone yet," he said with a wink.

Meanwhile, turbulence from the gusts was making it difficult for the helicopter to circle over the boat. Johnston and Murray struggled to keep the aircraft straight and level. Twice it was shoved down by wind shears, but it recovered both times just a few feet above the trees and power lines. Normally, with basket hoists, the chopper hovers at about 30 feet. But because of the turbulence, it remained at about 75 feet.

Using his handheld radio, Nettles told the crew that he was going to send the mother and the baby in the basket first, because the grandmother seemed to be in the best condition of the three. As the basket was being lowered, a gust caught the cable and blew it into one of the trees. The basket snagged on some branches, momentarily mooring the helicopter. Aware this could cause a catastrophe, Labeth quickly manipulated the hoist to create slack in the cable. Nettles freed the cable by snapping off branches and then guided the basket into the boat.

During the rescue, which was videotaped, Johnston radioed Nettles, "Noodles, you want me to come to the right?"

"No," Nettles replied. "Hold position . . . On deck, picking up slack [from the hoist line] . . . Waiting for survivor to get in basket . . . Hold position . . ." He helped Tasha, who was clutching Cassidy. Then Moreau handed him one of the dogs. "Woman and baby are getting into the basket . . ." He put the dog in the basket. "Ready for pickup . . . Picking up the slack . . . Start taking the load . . . Clear vessel . . . Clear back to the left . . ."

"Okay, can I move it to the right?" Johnston asked.

"Roger, that's fine . . . Basket's coming up . . . Basket is halfway up . . . Uh, she has a dog with her, too."

"That's fine, Noodles. Let her bring the dog. It's fine."

After Tasha and Cassidy were safely aboard, the basket was lowered again for Moreau. Holding a dog in each arm, she climbed in and was hoisted into the helicopter. Nettles then jumped in the water and attached himself to a safety device called a bear hook. As he was being pulled up, he saw animal carcasses, including a cow, float by.

After he was aboard, he did a medical assessment of the survivors and checked their pulses and blood pressure. Given what they had gone through, they were in good shape. Although shaken, the women were coherent and told him what had happened to them.

Concerned for the baby's well-being, Johnston decided to fly her to West Jefferson Medical Center in Marrero, south of New Orleans. But just minutes after the rescue, the crew spotted survivors who were waving at them from atop a levee. The helicopter landed, and Nettles jumped out to see if anyone needed medical attention. The survivors were in various stages of bewilderment and anguish and had swam or boated to the levee, which was the only landmark in the area that was above the floodwaters.

"Do you know of anyone else who might be trapped in their homes?" Nettles asked the stunned victims.

"I heard cries for help coming from somewhere down thataway," a woman said, pointing to a distant spot on the levee.

Nettles ran several hundred yards along the levee, sidestepping or hopping over swarms of snakes that had found refuge from the flood. He soon discovered the source of the shouting. About 150 yards from the levee, two men and their dog were sitting atop the roof of a partially collapsed house surrounded by water.

"Don't worry," Nettles shouted to them. "I'll get you out of there." He found a pirogue, but it didn't have a motor, pole, paddle, or oar. He hopped in it and, using his rescue swimmer fins as paddles, propelled the pirogue across the water to the stranded survivors.

The men and their dog squeezed into the pirogue with Nettles, who paddled back toward the levee. But the unstable, overloaded boat couldn't handle the weight. It began taking on water and then flipped over, spilling everyone. The boat was righted, and the men got back on. Nettles stayed in the water and put on his fins and then, pushing the pirogue from the stern, he flutter-kicked back toward the levee—with the frightened dog clinging to the rescue swimmer's back.

After the helicopter was loaded with survivors, Johnston called in more choppers to pick up the remaining people on the levee. On the 20-minute flight to West Jefferson Medical Center, Nettles was in awe at the devastation to the small fishing villages and communities of oil workers along the banks of the Mississippi. Battling stiff winds, Johnston expertly landed the aircraft on the helipad of the roof of the hospital's parking garage.

Tasha carried her baby into the hospital for a thorough examination, while Moreau—who had no purse, no money, and no shoes—sat on a curb outside and wept.

When the helicopter lifted off to pick up more survivors in Port Sulphur, Nettles gazed at the downtown area in New Orleans. From what he could see, it appeared to have weathered the storm. That was a big relief to him, because his wife, Angela, whom he had married a month earlier, was in the city at Tulane Medical Center, where she was a nurse in the pediatric intensive-care unit.

Thirty minutes after the first rescue, the crew learned that the levees had breached and that downtown was getting flooded and power was out. "We have our work cut out for us now," Nettles told his fellow Coasties.

They continued picking up survivors in the Port Sulphur area and bringing them to the hospital in Marrero. When the helicopter dropped off its latest group of survivors, a doctor told Nettles, "We can't take any more people. The hospital has no power or communications."

"You're taking them because they have nowhere else to go," Nettles insisted. "There's nothing you can do to stop us from bringing them here. They need help. You don't know how bad the situation is—and it's only going to get worse."

Then the crew began plucking people off rooftops and taking them to the Cloverleaf, a major interchange that was being used as a staging and evacuation center. From flying over the city, he now knew that the flood had reached Tulane Medical Center.

During one rescue, Nettles landed on a roof to hoist a skinny, elderly man. "Are you ready to go for a ride?" Nettles asked him.

"I can't leave my wife alone," the man responded. "She's still in the attic."

Nettles walked over to the side of a raised portion of the roof and peeked inside a hole. He saw a woman whom he estimated weighed more than 300 pounds. Staring at her and then the hole, he thought, *There's no way she can fit through that hole*. He radioed the crew, "I'm going to be here awhile. Send down a crash ax." He was asking for a blunt axlike instrument. For the next half hour, he bashed, banged, and pried siding and wood to make the hole bigger.

After all that work, he realized that she was too large to get through the framing in the attic and reach the hole. So he had to knock down several 2-foot-by-8-foot boards to clear a path for her. By this time, a rescue swimmer from another helicopter had come down to assist. After they helped the woman to the hole, they secured her to a strop and had her hoisted. Then Nettles put a strop around himself and her husband, and together they were brought up.

Nettles and his fellow Coasties were in full rescue mode—focused on saving one survivor at a time. He tried not to think about the huge number of people stranded in attics and rooftops. It was always the next person, the next hoist, the next flight.

The enormity of the disaster hit him hardest during the first night when victims by the thousands flicked on their flashlights signaling for help. *There are more lights below than stars in the sky*, he thought. Seeing all those little lights left him feeling sick to his stomach, as if someone had slugged him in the gut. *Oh my God, so many people need rescuing. It's overwhelming.* He shook his head. *Stop thinking about it. Get back into rescue mode. Just concentrate on the next rescue and the one after that. Don't think about anything else.* Still, it was hard not to worry about Angela, wondering how she was coping at her marooned hospital.

After an incredibly long and tiring day of nonstop rescues, Nettles and his fellow crewmen were ordered to rest. Nettles went into a broom closet at the damaged air station to get some sleep, but it took him an hour to calm down. Every time he closed his eyes, he kept seeing people on rooftops (a condition that went on for several months). After about four hours of sleep, he awoke and went back to his lifesaving work.

During one rescue the next day, he jumped in the polluted water and swam to a house to help evacuate a large number of survivors off a roof. On the flight to the drop-off zone, Nettles started to feel a burning sensation on his skin. "I need to go back to the base, fellas," he said. "I think I've got chemicals on me."

A crewmember called the base and said, "We need something there to help Noodles. He's suffering from chemical burns."

"We don't have any running water," came the reply. "Just bottles."

By the time the helicopter returned to the base, Nettles felt as if his skin from the neck down was on fire. The blades on the aircraft were still rotating when he jumped out and ran into a swampy ditch. He ripped off his short wetsuit and rubbed foul, murky swamp water over his body, trying to get the stinging chemicals off him. He managed, but his skin remained red like a bad sunburn for days.

Nettles shrugged off the discomfort, because he had a job to do. He spent his days on and off the cable, going down, going up, going down, going up, hour after hour in the scorching, humid weather. Sometimes he fastened a strop around himself and the survivor and was pulled up into the helicopter. Other times, he used the basket for the elderly and for children, especially when the kids were accompanied by a teenager or adult.

One time, the helicopter hovered over a two-story home where two teenagers were trapped. They had popped out an attic vent on the side of the house, which was large enough for a person to go through. To get inside, Nettles was lowered on the cable before he began swinging back and forth until he built up enough momentum to enter the hole. After putting the strop around himself and the first young person, Nettles stuck his head out of the hole and gave a thumbs-up signal to the flight mechanic. The second Nettles felt tension on the cable, he and the person leaped out of the hole and swung away from the house before being pulled up. Nettles repeated the rescue technique for the other teenager.

Nettles noticed most young children were suffering from shock to varying degrees as well as heat exhaustion, hunger, and thirst. Some kids were excited to be hoisted into a helicopter. To those who were fearful, Nettles calmly tried to set their minds at ease. "I'm going to put you in a basket and send you up to the helicopter," he told one terrified youngster. "It's going to be like a roller coaster ride."

"But I'm afraid of roller coasters," said the child.

"Ah, but this one is special," Nettles said. "This one is fun. You get to ride in a basket to a helicopter and fly over the city."

As the days wore on, Nettles sensed the desperation in survivors, especially those who felt they had been ignored.

When he was dropped onto the roofs of apartment buildings, where dozens of people were standing, he often found himself in a tense situation, because the helicopter could only carry four or five people at a time. "I can't take everyone," he would tell them. "Only those in medical need, the elderly, and children."

Some victims lied and claimed they had a medical condition. But when Nettles questioned them, they almost always gave wrong answers. In such cases, he made sure they were the last in the group to be rescued. After being threatened a couple of times by men wielding knives, he began carrying a crash ax with him when facing a crowd.

More often than not, though, Nettles and his fellow Coasties received *thank you*s from grateful survivors, who hugged and kissed them. He even got a big smooch on the cheek from an old, burly guy who smelled awful.

At the damaged coast guard air station, where crews were quartered between missions, Nettles felt the emotional pain suffered by rescue swimmers who dealt with heartbreaking fatalities. One rescue swimmer broke down when he recounted how he found several children on a rooftop next to their dead mother. He had to forcibly pick up the kids and put them in the helicopter, because they didn't want to leave the body behind. Another rescue swimmer was shaken after he went into a nursing home that had been abandoned by its caretakers. He found several bodies of elderly people who had dragged themselves out of their beds as the water rose, but fell and drowned.

One day, Nettles was lowered to a flooded residence where a severely dehydrated woman was lying unconscious. He could barely detect a pulse. Even though there were other people with her, he knew he didn't have time to hoist them up. "If I don't get her out of here right away, she's going to die," he told them. The helicopter whisked her to the hospital. Upon landing, Nettles didn't wait for a gurney but instead carried her into the emergency room. He never learned her fate.

During rooftop rescues, the rotor wash—the downward blast of air from the rotating blades of the helicopter—whipped up shingles, roofing tiles, nails, and other debris, which struck his bare legs and arms, cutting and scraping them. His helmet was getting battered, too. Although the wounds were minor, they became infected, because he spent time in the toxic floodwaters.

On the fifth day of the rescue operation, Nettles and fellow rescue swimmer David Foreman were ordered onto a Coast Guard Falcon jet that flew them to the air station in Mobile, Alabama, where they were given antibiotics. Nettles took his first hot shower in nearly a week and then he cut his hair short, hoping it would keep him cooler during his rescues.

The base's galley was closed because it was late, so the pair drove to the closest restaurant, a Golden Corral that was getting ready to lock its doors for the night. When the hostess learned they were Coasties who had come from Katrina rescues, she said, "Just grab some plates and eat at the buffet. And don't worry about paying for your meals." Although the remaining food was mostly dried-up meat or soggy vegetables that would have been tossed out, the men filled their plates. "This is the best meal I've had in my life," Nettles told Foreman.

Nettles slept in a comfy bed in an air-conditioned room. It felt glorious. Always in the back of his mind, though, was his worry for Angela at flooded and darkened Tulane Medical Center. Reaching her mother by phone, he broke down and cried with relief when he learned that Angela was safe and staying with her sister in Texas. Angela had been one of the last among the medical staff to evacuate the hospital, choosing to remain with the pediatric patients in the intensive-care unit until all were airlifted out.

Reassured that his bride was fine, Nettles returned to New Orleans with renewed vigor, doing what he loved—and was trained—to do: rescue people.

Less than a month after Katrina hit, Nettles and his fellow crewmen repeated their heroics by hoisting victims of Hurricane Rita to safety during heavy winds and rain.

Bobbie Jean Moreau; her daughter, Tasha Cheramie; and Tasha's infant daughter, Cassidy, were moved from the hospital to a shelter, where conditions were so bad they feared for the baby's life. They walked out and hitched a ride to a friend's house. Borrowing his truck, they left New Orleans and ended up staying with Moreau's nephew in Arkansas for several weeks before returning to the area. While her home was being repaired, Moreau lived in a camper trailer next door to one occupied by her daughter and granddaughter.

A year after their harrowing ordeal, they met three of their four rescuers in an emotional reunion at Air Station New Orleans during a special ceremony that honored more than 100 coast guard members for their efforts during the rescue operation. Nettles didn't meet the women, because he had been transferred to Air Station Los Angeles. However, he did exchange e-mails with Moreau.

After Los Angeles, Nettles was sent to Air Station North Bend (Oregon) and then was transferred to Air Station Cape Cod (Massachusetts), where, as of 2015, he was a chief aviation survival technician.

And what about his nickname, Noodles? Nettles explains: "When I was a new rescue swimmer, a friend and fellow Coastie, J. K. Smith, saw me doing something wild and crazy after work and he said, 'Nettles, you're not right in the noodle.' He thought for a moment and said, 'Hey, your new name is Noodles.' I hated it and said, 'Please don't call me that.' That was the wrong thing to say. The next day, everyone started calling me Noodles. I fought against it for a whole year, but the name stuck. Now I'm used to it—and I like it."

"THERE'S NO WAY WE'RE GOING TO DROWN"

Ashton Pruitt

As the threat of a watery death loomed over his family, 14-year-old Ashton Pruitt took charge. *There's no way we're going to drown,* he vowed to himself. *No way.*

After all, he was a Boy Scout, one who applied the famous Scout motto, "Be prepared," in his everyday life. Fortunately, he was prepared as the rising floodwaters from Hurricane Katrina trapped him and his family in their home.

The previous week, Ashton had attended a Boy Scout camp in Mississippi, where he learned emergency preparedness and water-safety skills and where he also proved he was a strong swimmer. Now he was faced with the challenge of putting what he had learned and practiced at camp to the test—a test that would determine whether he and his loved ones would live or die.

Although most people in the quaint, racially integrated, middle-class New Orleans neighborhood of Gentilly had evacuated before the storm, Ashton's family chose to stay behind in their peach-colored frame-and-brick house on Pasteur Boulevard. His mother, Deborah Pruitt; his 72-year-old grandmother, Lillian Brown; his legally blind 31-year-old brother, Charles Despenza; and his uncle, Wallace Young, were not concerned about the approaching hurricane. They thought so little of Katrina that they hadn't even bothered boarding up their home. However, at Ashton's insistence, the family had stocked up on bottled water, food, and flashlights and made sure their battery-powered radio was working.

Sunday night, the stiff winds and driving rain from the approaching hurricane began battering the New Orleans area. But Ashton figured there was little to fear, because his grandmother wasn't worried—and she had gone through Hurricane Betsy in 1965, an intense storm that killed 81 people. He had never experienced a major hurricane, so he found it somewhat exciting.

While he finished his homework, his family carried on as usual, chatting and watching TV. Weather forecasters on every local station were warning viewers that Katrina was an extremely dangerous storm that had the potential to create widespread damage. Then the power went out. To the family, the loss of electricity was a minor inconvenience. They continued to talk and joke until late into the night. Despite the noise from the howling wind and the sounds of flying debris crashing into the sides of houses, Ashton went to sleep.

After the hurricane cleared the area Monday morning, Ashton went outside to check the condition of the house. He was pleasantly surprised that he didn't find any signs of damage, not even a loose shingle. Elsewhere in the neighborhood, trees had been uprooted, parts of roofs blown off, and fences and utility poles knocked down.

To his family, it seemed the worst was over. No one knew that at 9:30 A.M., a dramatic event had unfolded that would soon put their lives in jeopardy. Just eight blocks away, two 30-foot-long sections of concrete floodwall of the London Avenue Canal had failed. The century-old levee that held back the canal burst open, sending torrents of water and sand into Gentilly. Storm-surge water gushed through the gaps, drowning several residents and destroying homes nearest the breaches. A wall of water plowed through the streets, flipping cars upside down, and lifting houses off their foundations and sending them crashing into nearby trees, utility poles, and buildings.

Ashton soon noticed out his window that the water was rising at an alarming rate. *That's strange*, he thought. *Where is this water coming from? And how high is it going to get?*

Listening to the radio, he heard the disturbing news about the breaches of the levees, not only of the ones at the London Avenue Canal but also major ruptures of the Industrial Canal a mile to the east of his house and the 17th Street Canal farther to the west. Other levees and canals had been topped by storm-surge waters. According to news reports, most of the city was experiencing, or would soon suffer, catastrophic flooding.

As the water rose at a frightening pace on Pasteur Boulevard, Ashton's mind began working in overdrive. Always thinking ahead because he was a "be prepared" kind of Boy Scout, he told himself, *We need to have a plan in case the water comes into the house.*

Ever since he had joined the Cub Scouts in second grade, Ashton had been hooked on scouting. When he was old enough, he became a Boy Scout and began earning merit badges in a variety of fields. Scouting opened his horizons and gave him the confidence to try anything and everything that interested him, from playing the piano to running track, from learning carpentry to weaving baskets. It also kept him out of trouble when other kids his age in the neighborhood were getting into mischief. By helping him stay challenged and focused, he became a stellar freshman student and athlete at Holy Cross High School in the city's Lower Ninth Ward.

He loved everything about scouting. As a Star Scout, which is the third-highest rank after Life and Eagle (the highest), he had earned an impressive number of merit badges and completed many hours of community service. He loved to learn new things and test his mental and physical abilities. That's why he thoroughly enjoyed the Scout camp in Mississippi with his fellow members of Troop 35, earning his swimming and emergency-preparedness merit badges.

Now, as the floodwaters were lapping against the front steps of his house, Ashton thought, *It can't possibly get much higher.* But it did. Then he began thinking about all the things he had absorbed the week before at the aquatics camp that were still fresh in his mind. He hoped he didn't need to put what he had learned to use—but he was glad he knew it.

Soon the water started seeping through the sides of the front door. When the water inside reached knee-high and showed no signs of slowing its steady rise, Ashton knew it was time to carry out an emergency-preparedness plan. "Let's get food, water, and supplies, and be ready to leave," he told his family. He grabbed some plastic garbage bags and filled them with canned goods, other nonperishable items, and bottled water. Another bag was stuffed with dry clothes for everyone. Meanwhile, his mother and grandmother were collecting treasured family photos and putting them in places that they hoped were high enough from the water.

Because they lived in a one-story house, Ashton didn't think the attic would provide them with a safe haven from the flood. "There's no telling how high the water will get," he told the family. "We can't go out onto the roof, because there isn't anywhere flat where we can sit or stand. The sides are too steep." He decided the safest place was the second-floor balcony of the house next door, which was unoccupied because the owners had evacuated. An overhang above the balcony offered some protection from the elements.

Ashton was aware that getting everyone out of the house and to safety would be a challenge. His grandmother was still recovering from knee surgery, and his brother, who could barely see, had a terrible fear of water.

Realizing that it would be difficult for family members to navigate the floodwaters, Ashton made flotation devices out of pants—a survival trick he had learned at Scout camp. With a pair of pants, he pulled up the zipper and tied off the end of each leg into a tight knot. Then he blew into the open waist so the legs filled up with air like balloons. Next, he tied off the waist and wrapped the air-filled pants around the neck of a family member. He made an improvised flotation device for each person.

With the water waist-high and still rising, he announced, "It's time to leave. If we try to open the front door, the water will rush in even worse than it is now. We'll have to go out a window." They chose a window in his bedroom on the left side of the house, because it was the closest to the neighbor's home.

But when they tried to open the window, it wouldn't budge. They discovered that all the windows were stuck shut from dried paint, because the house had recently been painted. Rather than bust out the glass, Ashton retrieved a martial arts sword from his karate class. He used the sword to cut the dried paint along the seam of the windowsill and opened the window.

Next, he went into a closet and brought out a foldable ladder. The 5-foot-6-inch teenager shoved it outside the window before jumping into the water. While grasping the ladder, he swam over to the neighbor's house and set up the ladder so it could reach the balcony.

The first person out of Ashton's house was his brother, Charles, who, despite his disability and fear of water, remained calm while Ashton gave him encouragement. Wearing one of Ashton's inflated pants around his neck to help keep his head above water, Charles grabbed hold of Ashton, who guided him to the neighbor's. Ashton then held on to the ladder until Charles reached the balcony.

Ashton's grandmother was next. Even though she had some physical limitations, she bravely made her way through the water with Ashton by her side. He helped her up the ladder. After she was safely on the balcony, the ladder slipped and plunged into the murky water.

"Mama, stay put until I find the ladder," Ashton shouted to his mother, who was getting ready to leave the house.

Ashton dived under the surface but couldn't locate the ladder, because it was hard to see in the deep floodwaters. The current was gaining strength and, he feared, had moved the ladder.

I have to find the ladder, he thought. *There's no way I can get Mama and Uncle Wallace up to the balcony without it. Maybe I can reach the bottom if I jump off the balcony.* During the previous week at the Scout camp, one of his requirements to obtain a merit badge was to dive into water over his head and retrieve an object at the bottom. Now he had to do basically the same thing, only the stakes were much higher. Lives of loved ones were at risk.

He climbed the neighbor's porch to the balcony and leaped off. He touched bottom and felt around with his bare feet but failed to find the ladder. Again and again, he scaled the porch and jumped, trying to recover the ladder. With each leap into the water, he could feel an ever-heightening sense of desperation. Finally, after the tenth attempt, his toes brushed up against the ladder. *I found it!*

He set up the ladder again and called for his mother to leave the house. Clutching the flotation device that Ashton had fashioned, his mother swam to the ladder and went up to the balcony. His uncle also made it without any further problems.

When everyone was safe and the garbage bags of supplies and dry clothes were brought up to the balcony, Ashton relaxed. He was so relieved that he began swimming around in the flood just for the fun of it. *This is pretty cool!* he thought. *When will I ever have another chance to swim in the neighborhood? Never.* He was enjoying the whole experience so much that he wasn't thinking about death and destruction.

It was such a weird sensation for him. Here he was, swimming more than 10 feet above the streets where just days earlier he rode his bike and roller-skated and played basketball. After about ten minutes of frolicking in the water, Ashton heard his mother shout to him, "That's enough. Come on and get up here where it's safe."

He climbed onto the balcony and looked around. His neighborhood was one big lake. The water was 13 feet deep and still rising. Some houses were completely submerged while the only thing visible on others was a roof barely sticking above the surface. Ashton didn't see any people. It was as if he and his family were the only ones left in all of Gentilly.

But then, from somewhere in the distance, they heard an old woman scream for help. Many residents were elderly people who knew Ashton because he sometimes did little chores for them. He wondered if the screaming woman was someone who had bought church raffle tickets or bags of Boy Scout popcorn from him.

He wanted to try to find her and save her. But his family wouldn't let him leave, believing it was too dangerous for him to swim in the polluted, swiftly moving floodwaters. If only he knew where the pleading voice was coming from, Ashton figured, he could talk the family into letting him go after her. But in the otherwise creepy quietness that had enveloped the neighborhood, what few sounds there were carried a great distance, so there was no way to know the woman's location.

Ashton felt frustrated that there was nothing he could do for her or anybody else. He, like the rest of the family, figured their best option was to sit tight and wait for help to show up. They didn't know if that would take a few hours, a few days, or even longer.

At least his family was safe thanks to his Boy Scout training. And knowing that gave him some consolation for the predicament they were in. Looking on the bright side, he said, "We have food, water, dry clothes, and a dry place above the flood. The sun is out, too. We're lucky and blessed."

"We're lucky and blessed because you were with us, Ashton," his mother replied.

"I wasn't going to let anything bad happen to us," he said, adding, "not if I could help it."

Late in the afternoon, a military helicopter flew by and hovered over them. But because of downed trees and power lines by the house, there was no safe way for the helicopter to lower a rescue basket. Seeing that the family looked in good shape, the pilot flew off.

"Well, at least they know we are here," Ashton said. Later that evening, another helicopter flew by and shined a spotlight on the family. But once again, the pilot determined it was too risky to attempt a rescue and left the area.

Despite their obvious disappointment over the flybys, Ashton and his family remained in good spirits, because they weren't suffering any major distress or discomfort. However, Ashton was still bothered by those occasional distant screams for help, which were growing weaker and further apart by the hour.

Eventually, the family fell asleep under the stars. The next morning, the water had risen to 18 feet and leveled off. Ashton no longer heard any screams for help from the old lady. He hoped that was a sign she had been rescued, but he suspected her silence meant something else—that she had died.

Soon, a pleasure boat commandeered by firefighters showed up and took Ashton and his family to the campus of the University of New Orleans, which was about a half mile away. Even though the school was located on the banks of Lake Pontchartrain and was bordered on the west by the London Avenue Canal, it sat on high ground, so most of it wasn't flooded. About 200 to 300 survivors had made their way to the campus, but there was no one in authority to assist them.

People of all ages were milling around, many still shell-shocked by the flooding. Some survivors suffered minor injuries and were being treated by a few overwhelmed medical technicians who themselves were victims. Having earned a merit badge in first aid and emergency preparedness, Ashton volunteered to help, and so did his mother. Together, they helped treat people with bad cuts and scrapes.

Later in the day, a helicopter picked up Ashton and his family and brought them to a causeway that was being used as a staging area for evacuations out of the city. After waiting for seven hours, the family boarded a bus that took them to Houston, Texas, where they and thousands of other survivors were given shelter in the Astrodome. The family temporarily settled in Houston.

When the Boy Scouts of America learned of Ashton's valor and resourcefulness in keeping his family alive during the flood, the organization awarded him the prestigious Honor Medal with Crossed Palms "for unusual heroism and extraordinary skill or resourcefulness in saving or attempting to save lives at extreme risk to self."

At the award ceremony, Ashton's mother, Deborah Pruitt, told Scout officials, "Without the training Ashton received, we would not have survived."

Ashton, who admitted he was humbled by the award, said at the time, "In the moment, I wasn't really thinking about what could happen to my family. I was just thinking about protecting the people that I love."

Because his home was severely damaged by the flood, Ashton spent his sophomore year of high school in Houston. Eventually, he and his family returned to New Orleans, where they lived in a FEMA trailer in their front yard for 16 months while their house was being repaired with the help of volunteers.

Ashton went back to Holy Cross High School and graduated in 2009. During this time, he rejoined Troop 35 and achieved the rank of Eagle Scout.

In 2015, Ashton was attending Our Lady of Holy Cross College in New Orleans, studying for a degree in psychology and working part-time as a lifeguard at a swimming center.

Says Ashton, "One of the most important lessons I learned from Hurricane Katrina was to be strong in a time of need."

"IT'S LIKE THE END OF DAYS"

Dr. Scott Delacroix

Late in the night, about 48 hours after Hurricane Katrina had churned away, Dr. Scott Delacroix, Jr., stopped his car at a major New Orleans interchange of overpasses and ramps. He did a double take. "What in the world?" he mumbled to himself.

Under the glare of portable road-construction lights, he stared at several thousand evacuees crowded behind police barricades as helicopters landed and took off. Grim-faced men, women, and children—many in mud-caked, flood-soaked clothes—were ambling mindlessly in a state of shock amid garbage that was strewn everywhere.

On the eastbound lanes, patients by the hundreds were slumped in wheelchairs, sprawled on stretchers, and hunched on pieces of cardboard. Elderly people were lying on gurneys or on the concrete with hospital medical charts jammed under their heads or feet. Some were in hospital gowns and adult diapers; others in bathrobes and pajamas.

To Delacroix (pronounced DELLA-crow), a 26-year-old urologist, it looked like he had come upon a refugee camp in a third-world country. Only worse. It was hard for him to fathom that this was the Cloverleaf—where I-10 meets Causeway Boulevard—which normally was one of the city's busiest interchanges. But times now were anything but normal.

He bolted out of his car to assess the situation. The Cloverleaf had been turned into an emergency staging area for first responders to bring rescued hurricane survivors as well as patients from flooded hospitals and nursing homes. Every few minutes, military helicopters landed and delivered a new bunch of dazed victims who joined the thousands of others who had been waiting—some for nearly two days—to be moved to shelters in buses that had yet to show up. They had little or no water or food.

Talking to the few overworked nurses and medics who were treating the neediest with limited medical supplies, Delacroix asked, "So, who is in charge?"

After learning he was a doctor, one of the nurses replied, "You are."

Born and raised in the New Orleans area, Scott Delacroix was a second-year resident at Charity Hospital downtown. Because he wasn't on call when the storm approached, he drove to Madisonville, a small town on the north shore of Lake Pontchartrain, to keep his father company after his mother and two siblings had evacuated. The family house stood up well against Katrina, unlike the surrounding pine trees that the winds knocked down, blocking streets throughout the area. For the next day and a half, Delacroix wielded a chainsaw to help clear driveways and roads. He used chains and his SUV, an old but trusty Toyota 4Runner with nearly 200,000 miles on the odometer, to pull the trees out of the way.

Late Wednesday afternoon, he was listening to WWL, one of the few area radio stations still able to broadcast. He heard a live phone interview with friend and fellow doctor London Guidry, a surgical resident at Charity Hospital. She said that hundreds of patients and medical staff were trapped inside by the flood. They had no running water, no electricity, and no help from the outside world. The staff, she added, was doing all it could to keep suffering patients alive, but she feared for everyone's safety because of reports of looting, shootings, and attacks on rescue personnel.

I need to make my way back there, Delacroix thought. *I have to help them.*

He donned blue medical scrubs and a white lab coat which held medicine in one pocket and bullets in the other for the .38-caliber pistol he took with him—just in case. After he loaded up and gassed his car, he headed for New Orleans. Normally, it was a 45-minute trip to downtown where the hospital was located. But because the Lake Pontchartrain Causeway and sections of I-10 were closed and other roads were blocked by debris and high water, it took several hours just to get close to the city. By then it was night.

The first few roadblocks Delacroix encountered were manned by police, who drew their weapons on him until he identified himself. They told him that power and communications were out and that the city was extremely dangerous, because gun stores had been looted and criminals were now heavily armed. Although police were ordered to keep people from entering New Orleans, Delacroix was able to convince them to let him pass, because he was a doctor wanting to get to Charity Hospital. Unsettled by having weapons pointed at him, he tried a new tactic. As he neared the next few roadblocks, Delacroix turned off his headlights and put on his inside lights so the police could see that a doctor was in the vehicle.

No matter which street he tried, floodwaters were too deep for him to get near Charity. Eventually, he found his way onto I-10 in Kenner, a few miles west of the city, and headed toward the darkened downtown. *This is eerie*, he thought, driving on the lonely interstate. *No lights anywhere. No police. No military. No cars. No people.*

Suddenly, he came upon the chaos at the lit-up Cloverleaf where about 20 state troopers were trying to deal with 3,000 overwrought survivors. Helicopters were landing on the westbound lanes, depositing evacuees who were then hustled across the median to join others behind police barricades.

Delacroix parked his car and entered a world more suited to a disturbing scene in a disaster movie than this real-life calamity of confusion, disorganization, and suffering. He hurried over to where an emergency room doctor, two psychologists, a neurologist, several nurses, and ambulance medics had set up a makeshift triage area under an overpass. Scurrying from one patient to another, the besieged medical personnel had few supplies and were unable to handle the huge volume of patients, many in critical condition. As a result, the weak and dying who had been lying in the oppressive heat for two days were struggling to hang on.

With no one officially in charge, Delacroix stepped in. *This is where I'm supposed to be*, he told himself. Wherever he looked, he saw sick and injured people. *It's a highway of patients.* Walking down the eastbound lane of I-10, he began examining patients, some too feeble to speak, their heads resting on their medical charts. Caught in a steady flow of patients of all ages, he had to deal with elderly persons complaining of chest pain and shortness of breath . . . preschoolers suffering seizures . . . asthmatics and emphysema victims seeking oxygen and respiratory treatment . . . evacuees experiencing dehydration . . . mentally disabled people unwilling to cooperate. The number of patients kept growing as helicopters kept landing.

Because only three oxygen tanks were available, patients had to wait to receive oxygen therapy while hoping they could hold out before their frail lungs quit. Supplies were so low that Delacroix was wiping off ventilation masks and reusing them.

In a nonstop procession, patients came under their own power or were carried to the triage area. Some clutched their medical charts from whichever hospital they had been evacuated. Many could be treated on the spot, such as giving insulin to diabetics and bandaging patients who had cut their hands or legs trying to escape their attics.

But other cases were more complex. Delacroix examined a patient who had undergone open-heart surgery several days earlier and still had chest tubes in him. *I can't believe he was evacuated here*, the doctor thought. *This is someone's parent who had been safe in a hospital but is now in our care, lying on a highway exposed to the elements. It's not right.*

Delacroix took a moment to gaze at the rows of patients waiting to be seen. *What is going on in their minds?* he wondered. *How worried are they that they'll survive?* Spotting a delirious mental patient who was clad in a diaper, the doctor thought, *He has no clue where he is, and in this case, that's probably a blessing. This situation can't go on for much longer. Surely, officials will bring in transportation and get these people out of here soon.*

Delacroix turned his attention back to triage, which meant a quick 15-second reading of a patient's medical chart to determine the severity of his or her condition. He graded patients on a scale of one to three, with one receiving top priority for the next available ambulance. Few vehicles had shown up, but around 2 A.M., a line of ambulances from Acadian Ambulance Service arrived to transport the most critical patients to the airport terminal's temporary FEMA-run medical facility or to hospitals in Baton Rouge.

Sometimes Delacroix had to delay moving a patient who had been lying on the median for more than 24 hours so that another person in worse shape could go first. Occasionally, he had to split up families, because there wasn't room in the ambulance. His rule was one family member with each patient for the ride. When an epileptic child was losing consciousness, Delacroix put her and her mother in an ambulance, leaving the woman's other three children with their 70-year-old grandmother. There was nothing else he could do for them.

While conducting triage, he saw that Nick Pieper, a volunteer who had recently finished his emergency medical technician training, was squeezing by hand a ventilator that was connected to a child with cystic fibrosis. The child's battery-powered ventilator had run out of juice. Delacroix ordered the child put in the next available ambulance.

The doctor noticed that for every patient taken away by ambulance, ten more survivors were arriving at the Cloverleaf on a helicopter. Although most were healthy, many weren't. Delacroix often went into the crowd to figure out who needed medical care and who didn't. Most evacuees were tired, thirsty, angry, and upset, but that wasn't a good enough reason to receive medical care or get a ride in an ambulance. The most critical cases were airlifted out by Black Hawk helicopters, which could be packed with up to 14 patients each.

While examining evacuees, the doctor was repeatedly interrupted with medical emergencies like persons who had collapsed from acute chest pains. When a young man suffered a horrible asthma attack that was so bad his family feared he would die, the doctor administered oxygen and used a nebulizer, a device that turns liquid medicine into a mist for people who have trouble breathing. The quick treatment ended the crisis. In another case, he had to stick an IV of fluids into a two-year-old who was so dehydrated his diaper had been dry for two days.

Although cell-phone service seldom worked, a psychologist who was helping triage patients got through to an official in Baton Rouge. Given the phone, Delacroix told the official, "We need Pedialyte [a liquid that replaces lost body fluids], baby formula, oxygen, aspirin, IV sedation, and also nitroglycerin. I'm rationing two bottles of it. And we desperately need transportation. People are dying out here because we can't get them to hospitals."

FEMA had arranged for buses to take evacuees to shelters in other cities. But there were so few buses that they barely made a dent in the growing mass of arriving survivors. Although Delacroix was heartened to see some victims leave this hellish area, he was saddened by the extreme selfishness displayed by the strong and the healthy. With concern only for themselves, they pushed and shoved women, children, and the elderly out of the way in the mad scramble to board the buses. The few state police on hand were powerless to stop it. The weak soon gave up even trying to get on, and some just laid down and waited to die. By early morning, several bodies had been covered and placed in the median behind a medical trailer that had been brought in.

When dawn broke on Thursday, Delacroix was glad it was overcast. Some people had been at the Cloverleaf with little provisions for nearly three days and had suffered under the blazing sun. "Hold on just a little longer," he'd tell them. "The bus should be here to take you away within an hour or two." He was tired of lying to evacuees, tired of giving them false hope.

Ambulances were arriving more frequently to transport patients, and more buses were showing up. But again, getting the elderly and large families aboard was problematic because of all the pushing and shoving from younger, more aggressive survivors.

Walking over to those who were standing around in the sweltering heat and muddy sides of the interstate, he began inviting families with children to sit under the shady overpass. *They're not going to make it onto a bus as a family anyway—if enough buses ever show up*, he thought.

Later that morning, ten members of the Austin Emergency Medical Services (EMS) arrived with a command-and-control trailer and four ambulances. Delacroix told them to set up a triage unit on the opposite side of the Cloverleaf. Meanwhile, helicopters continued to drop off victims. By now, the number of survivors at the site had swelled to about 4,000 with no end in sight.

Then Delacroix received word that FEMA, which was in charge of transportation, was pulling out of the Cloverleaf. He approached a FEMA official and asked, "Why are you leaving?"

The official shrugged and replied, "I don't know. The decision was made by people above my pay grade. I think it has to do with reports of shootings in New Orleans."

"That's ridiculous," the doctor said. "We're a mile and a half outside the city proper. There's been no gunfire here, and we haven't had any security problems. But I guarantee you we will have some serious ones if you stop the buses and ambulances from picking up the people. They've been stuck out here for days without proper food and water. The lack of transportation will cause more of them to become medical patients because of dehydration and exhaustion. Patients are lying on the interstate in their own urine and feces. Medical supplies are still minimal."

The official said, "Sorry. There's nothing I can do about it." Then he walked away. The military helicopters, meanwhile, continued to unload survivors and deliver bottles of water and MREs.

As anger and frustration built up in Delacroix, he faced an annoying situation. A large hungry pit bull—apparently an abandoned pet that had found its way to the Cloverleaf—had been scaring patients and the medical workers for several hours. The doctor found a bottle containing tranquilizer pills. He rolled one of the pills into a piece of cheese from an MRE and fed it to the dog. A short while later, the pit bull was passed out on the grass and didn't wake up until the next morning.

Austin EMS took over the triage responsibility while Delacroix and several medical workers tried to clean up the area, which had turned into a disgusting clutter of trash and human waste. Helpless people had urinated and defecated where they stood while waiting for transportation. The doctor cut holes in several cloth cots and placed boxes under them so patients could relieve themselves.

During the day, Delacroix bumped into one of his former Charity Hospital patients, who said he had been evacuated from a senior citizens apartment complex near Bayou St. John. "There are still about a hundred and fifty seniors back there without water," he told the doctor. "They're beyond desperate."

Delacroix spoke with an air-traffic controller (ATC) from the Kentucky Air National Guard who was directing helicopter traffic in and out of the Cloverleaf. "I need a chopper to bring supplies to stranded seniors," the doctor told him. Several hours later, a Black Hawk was loaded with bottles of water and MREs. After donning bulletproof vests, Delacroix; Pieper, an emergency room doctor from Baton Rouge; two Austin medics; and four state police officers armed with AR-15 semiautomatic rifles hopped into the helicopter.

Before it took off at around 6 P.M., Delacroix told Pieper, "This is the first, and I hope only, time I'll be seeing patients with a bulletproof vest on, a .38 revolver in my scrub pants, and .38-caliber cartridges jingling in my coat pocket."

As they flew over the city, the doctor was astounded by the vastness of the destruction and flooding. He could hardly believe so much of his hometown was underwater. Within minutes, the Black Hawk hovered over the apartment building, but the pilot determined it wasn't safe to land on the roof. Instead, he put down at a softball field two blocks away.

After finding some abandoned pirogues, the group filled them with supplies and waded through 3-foot-deep water to the senior citizens complex. Help came too late for a few who had died. After examining and treating those with serious health issues, the group returned to the landing zone after nightfall. But the helicopter was gone.

One of the state troopers contacted his commander by radio and was told that it was unlikely a helicopter would land at the softball field because of reports of gunfire. Getting increasingly nervous, the men popped glow sticks and arranged them in a pattern, hoping to catch the attention of any pilot. Later, a chopper attempted to land, but three gunshots from across the bayou scared it off. Using a dugout as a bunker, the men remained stranded for about four hours before a Black Hawk, flying without lights and with a crew using night-vision goggles, picked them up and returned them to the Cloverleaf.

Delacroix was dismayed to see that the triage area was as busy as ever. There was still no sign of FEMA. Meanwhile, Austin EMS was ordered to pack up and head to the airport to help staff the temporary medical facility there.

Exhausted beyond what they thought possible, Delacroix and Pieper took a break from the Cloverleaf and, at about 1 A.M. Friday morning, drove to the airport in the 4Runner to help out. The doctor was shocked by what he saw: On the first floor of the stuffy main terminal, it was so crammed that patients—including many he had treated the day earlier—were sitting or lying on the floor in the baggage-claim area and outside on the concrete passenger drop-off zone.

Delacroix and Pieper strode up to the second floor where FEMA had set up its medical station. The duo introduced themselves and offered their services, but officials turned them down, claiming, "You're not government-accredited personnel. You aren't certified as being part of this triage unit."

"But we've been treating people at the Cloverleaf," Delacroix argued. "Many of them were brought here and are still waiting downstairs."

"We're working as fast as we can," the official said. "Thank you for your offer, but we can't have any civilians assisting us. Only first responders certified by the government can be in here."

The pair looked at each other in frustration. After expressing to the official their extreme displeasure over the bureaucracy and the deplorable conditions at the airport, the two left. As they walked back to the car, Delacroix told Pieper, "I feel terrible that this is where our patients ended up. I had told them they were being transported to a medical facility, because that's what I believed. All the government is doing is flying them four miles to the airport where they're just left alone. The entire evacuation process is completely screwed up."

They drove to Baton Rouge for some much needed sleep. At 11 A.M. Friday, they went to the emergency operations center, where they loaded up the 4Runner with medical supplies.

There was still no word on the fate of the medical staff at Charity Hospital.

When the pair returned to the Cloverleaf that afternoon, the number of survivors there had ballooned to more than 5,000, many of them bewildered, fatigued, and hot. FEMA had yet to resume transportation to evacuate them on a large scale. Police from other states had arrived to maintain some semblance of control.

Confronting two FEMA officials, Delacroix demanded to know, "Where are the buses?"

"That's not our responsibility at the moment," replied one of them. "We're here only to pick up bodies of the deceased."

"Incredible," Delacroix scoffed. "You're here to help the dead but not the living. Unbelievable."

Turning to Pieper, he said, "How could this be happening in my city in the greatest country on Earth? It's been four days since the hurricane and still no FEMA presence here. This is outrageous. Nick, I need to see something other than poor people herded like cattle under the interstate."

They drove about two miles south to where Airline Highway was flooded. They joined a police officer, judge, and an armed man and boarded a 20-foot pleasure craft in search of people still stranded in their homes in the Carrollton area. On almost every other block, they spotted a dead body—usually an elderly person—floating in the putrid water, caught in a downed tree, or snagged on a fence. One of the bodies was directly across the street from Delacroix's favorite Chinese restaurant. "It's like the End of Days," he told Pieper.

The group stopped at several flooded houses where people

were sitting on their front porch. Some refused to leave despite Delacroix's warning, "This is your best shot at getting out of here." If they declined his offer, he didn't press the issue unless they had children with them. "You must get the kids out," he stressed. "Keeping them here is not safe and it's not right. They deserve hot meals and running water and health care."

About half the time, the survivors agreed to be rescued. After collecting 15 persons on the boat and bringing them to dry land, the pair returned to the Cloverleaf. Delacroix's heart sank when he saw there were more evacuees now than ever before. Rows of people 30 deep were lined along I-10 for about 300 yards—the equivalent of three football fields. It reminded him of crowds at Mardi Gras parades but without the smiling faces and colorful beads.

His first patient that afternoon was a woman with six children and her elderly mother. "It's been hell on earth," she told him. "My family and I have been here since Wednesday. Please let us come sit over here in the medical area."

"Of course," he said. *This is really sad*, he thought. *For a woman to beg to sit among dying people and near the excrement of patients who've been left here for days says a lot about the condition of this place.*

Friday evening, Delacroix treated a woman who had gone into labor. Hoping he wouldn't have to deliver the baby under such terrible conditions, Delacroix put the woman and her six-year-old son on the next outbound helicopter. Joining them for the short flight to Ochsner Medical Center, he monitored her condition until they landed in the back parking lot, where she was turned over to the care of ER doctors. He then caught a ride with a police officer who drove him back to the Cloverleaf. He later learned the woman delivered a healthy child.

Delacroix began treating more patients for anxiety. "Oh, everything is going to be okay," he'd tell them. "The buses and ambulances are coming." *When is it going to be okay?* he asked himself. *When are those buses coming? Where is FEMA?*

Some of the same people who were here on Tuesday were still here. Emotions were running high. Meanwhile, helicopters continued delivering evacuees.

Delacroix expressed his frustration to the air-traffic controller who had become his friend. "The Cloverleaf is getting out of hand, and there's going to be trouble," the doctor warned. "Evacuees need to be taken somewhere other than here, and the ones here need to be transported out."

A half hour later, the ATC told Delacroix, "Doc, good news. We're starting a massive evacuation with helicopters and buses."

"That's great," Delacroix said. "Where are the people going?"

"The airport."

Delacroix rolled his eyes. "Well, I guess it's better than here."

"We need you to help organize everyone into lines."

Shortly after midnight, Operation Cloverleaf—a military airlift involving Black Hawk and the larger Chinook helicopters—got under way. All medical care ceased so that Delacroix, medics, and Guardsmen could coordinate the evacuation.

The sickest patients were transported out first. Delacroix helped organize families so they could remain together when they boarded the helicopters. Those who were afraid to fly were given a sedative to calm them.

He gave special attention to a family of eight. The parents' son, Kendall, had been a former patient of his who had died of a cancerous tumor three years earlier. While attending medical school at that time, Delacroix had been Kendall's "big buddy" at Children's Hospital and had grown close to the family. He was heartsick when he saw them suffering at the Cloverleaf. The only item they had salvaged from their flooded home was a photo of Kendall. The doctor wrapped the picture in a plastic bag and ushered the family to the front of the line and made sure they boarded the same helicopter together.

Even though officials said pets weren't allowed on the flights, Delacroix paid no attention to the ban. He stuffed lap dogs in boxes and helped hide cats in bags, reminding grateful pet owners, "Don't tell anyone about your pet until you get somewhere safe."

During the wee hours, Delacroix stood in his socks in a soggy field because the mud sucked his shoes right off his feet. Using a bullhorn, he directed evacuees to the helicopters, which were landing two and three at a time every five to ten minutes. The EMTs batched families together and waited for a signal from Delacroix on how many people to send to the next available chopper.

Around 4 A.M., he received word that all patients and

personnel at Charity Hospital had been evacuated. *What a relief*, he thought. *My friends are safe.*

At dawn, a convoy of buses arrived. Between the buses and the helicopters, the number of evacuees remaining on the Cloverleaf shrank dramatically. By 11 A.M., the only ones milling around at the smelly, trashy interchange were a few dozen military personnel, medics, Delacroix, and several dogs and cats that had been left behind.

With his ears ringing from the noise of the helicopters, Delacroix plopped down on a cot next to several fellow volunteers. He was fatigued, but the adrenaline that had been coursing through his body over the past hours kept him awake. "This whole week has been surreal," he said. "The government response to this disaster has been horrible. It's as if the feds didn't care about the people who were stuck here." He glanced at Pieper and male nurses Kelly Tourere, Danny Dickson, Jay Seymore, Scott McCain, and a small cadre of LSU medical students who all had worked long, strenuous hours trying to ease the suffering of the victims at the Cloverleaf. "If nothing else," Delacroix told them, "I hope the survivors know that we cared."

Saturday afternoon, Delacroix and Pieper returned to the airport and again offered their assistance at the FEMA-run medical station in the terminal, which was overflowing with evacuees and patients. But, like before, the pair was spurned, because they weren't certified by the government.

Knowing that search teams in boats were still rescuing people in flooded neighborhoods, Delacroix and Pieper set up a triage area Sunday at an I-10 exit in east New Orleans where they examined 400 people. The aluminum street light poles had been cut down so helicopters could land safely and pick up the survivors. The next day, the pair triaged about 50 people out of the back of the doctor's 4Runner.

With federal forces finally in control of the situation, Delacroix headed home. He was supposed to return to his post at Charity the following morning, but it was no longer a functioning hospital.

He completed his residency at LSU and Ochsner Clinic in 2009 and did a three-year fellowship in urologic oncology at MD Anderson Cancer Center at the University of Texas. He is now director of urologic oncology at Louisiana State University Medical Center and also practices in New Orleans and nearby Metairie.

"I don't think about Katrina on a daily basis," Delacroix says. "But it's always in the back of my mind. For a long time I had trouble believing that it had happened. I lost confidence in the government response to a disaster, because Katrina didn't just over-whelm the system, it broke it. I hope the government and the people of the city of New Orleans have learned from this and will do better with the next disaster."

"I MUST RESCUE THOSE ANIMALS"

Jane Garrison

From the comfort of her home in Charleston, South Carolina, Jane Garrison was glued to the TV set, watching live coverage of the human misery, destruction, and flooding in the wake of Hurricane Katrina. The news was upsetting her. She couldn't eat or sleep. And although she felt great sympathy for the suffering of people who were displaced and for those who lost loved ones, Garrison's heart was breaking for the other victims—the tens of thousands of pets that were left behind.

The animal crisis flared up because evacuees weren't allowed to take their cats, dogs, and other pets to shelters. Many owners left food and water for their animals before departing, figuring that once the storm passed, they would reunite with their pets in two or three days. No one ever imagined that they wouldn't be able to go home—if their home was still standing or inhabitable—for weeks or months.

Many of those people who chose to ride out the hurricane with their pets became trapped in attics and rooftops by the flood and needed to be rescued. But authorities wouldn't let victims bring their animals to emergency shelters or on to evacuation buses. As a result, once-pampered dogs and sweet house cats were abandoned at home, in yards, or on roadsides.

Through her tears, Garrison was seeing TV footage and Internet images of loveable pets turning into skittish, fearful animals struggling alone in unfamiliar and dangerous surroundings . . . of strays clinging to floating debris . . . of dogs chained to front porches or left on rooftops of flooded houses. She was hearing reports that thousands upon thousands of animals were trapped in homes in extreme heat without access to fresh water or food.

It was too much to bear for Garrison, a longtime animal advocate and certified disaster rescuer. She had helped save animals in the aftermath of floods in California and tornadoes in Arkansas and also ran an international campaign for six years to protect elephants.

So when a fellow advocate phoned her from New Orleans and complained that little was being done to save abandoned and homeless animals, Garrison, then 37, sprang into action. "I can't take it any longer," she told her husband, Mark. "I have to do something. I must rescue those animals."

Garrison loaded her SUV with pet carriers, traps, and pet supplies. She also packed PowerBars, water, a sleeping bag, and sturdy work gloves. Then she drove 14 straight hours to Gonzales, Louisiana—about 60 miles northwest of New Orleans—where state officials and the Louisiana Society for the Prevention of Cruelty to Animals (LA/SPCA) had set up an animal rescue shelter at the Lamar Dixon Expo Center. The facility was normally an equestrian complex, but it was turned into a shelter and staging area for what would become the largest animal rescue operation in United States history.

At first, the LA/SPCA had collected a modest list of addresses from evacuees who had left their pets behind, so Garrison joined one of the few four-person teams to rescue those animals. It was incredibly hot and humid in the disaster zone. Every breath she took reminded her that the stagnant air was thick and stinky.

Although members of her team were reluctant to break into locked houses, she reminded them that it was the only way to save the pets. In her first rescue, they broke a window so Garrison could crawl inside. She followed the sounds of meowing and found a skinny black cat in the bathroom with her kittens.

Garrison and her rescue partners went to other houses on the list. Although they were successful in saving several pets, she knew that in a metropolitan area of more than one million people, there were tens of thousands of animals waiting to be rescued. *It's overwhelming*, she thought. *We need more volunteers.*

After the first week of her mission, Garrison dictated an e-mail to her husband and asked him to send it out to everyone they knew. Her e-mail said, in part, "I am on the front lines. We need people down here, because these animals are going to die unless we rescue them. Please, please, get on a plane or get in your car. Come with crowbars, carriers, leashes, bowls."

Hundreds of pet lovers and volunteers from animal-welfare agencies, rescue leagues, and humane societies throughout the country responded to Garrison's plea or had decided on their own to help. Within 2 days, Garrison was organizing more than 300 volunteers. By now, thousands of phone calls and e-mails were pouring in from evacuees who were scattered across the country wanting their pets rescued. The list of addresses grew to more than 7,000. But Garrison knew that an untold number of animals were trapped in other residences of owners who, for various reasons, hadn't called authorities.

Day after day, Garrison, wearing jeans inside hip waders and a sweat-soaked T-shirt, slogged through flooded streets, calling out, "Puppy! Kitty!" She often heard instant replies—usually muffled barking coming from boarded-up houses, although from her vantage point, it was hard to tell exactly where. She knew that for every dog that was barking, there was a cat somewhere confined in a home that wasn't being heard.

So Garrison went door-to-door, knocking on the sides of houses, listening for signs of life. Whenever she heard barking inside a home, she used a crowbar to pry the plywood off a boarded-up window and then smashed the glass before entering a nightmarish scene. Rooms were dark, stuffy, and steamy. Mold was growing on the walls and floors. The smell of rotten food and sometimes the decomposing body of a dead animal made her gag.

But Garrison's breaking and entering sometimes caused an already freaked-out animal inside to panic and hide or snarl and stand its ground. *Animals know something isn't right, that their lives are in danger*, she told herself. *They need comfort from a soft human voice, a gentle touch.* Speaking in a calm, loving manner, she usually could sweet-talk the helpless, traumatized animal to come to her.

But with some pets, especially cats, it was much harder if they didn't want to be found. Frightened felines had a knack for hollowing out box-spring mattresses and the bottoms of couches to hide. Garrison had to pull covers off beds or look under mattresses, sofas, and chairs. If she and her rescue partners couldn't find the pet, they moved on, because there were so many other animals that needed to be saved. Every time she walked out of a pet owner's house without finding the animal, she felt heartbroken. All she could do was leave a door or window open so the pet could get out on its own. *At least it'll have a fighting chance of surviving or of having someone else find it*, she reasoned.

Just as often, Garrison encountered pets that needed no coaxing at all. More than once, she smashed a window to gain entry into a house and found a dog or cat that couldn't leap into her arms fast enough.

Garrison was so focused on trying to rescue animals that she didn't pay attention to the toxic makeup of the muck and water or reports of deadly snakes lurking in the flooded streets. As she waded through the water, her main concern was her footing. Many manhole covers had been blown open by the flood, so she had to watch each step to avoid a sudden plunge down a sewer hole. She also had to look out for submerged downed utility poles, branches, wire fences, and sharp-edged pieces of debris that could trip her up.

Some people had urged her to wear a mask because she was being exposed to mold, mildew, and foul air in the houses, but she refused. "If you know animals," she explained, "then you know dogs and cats can be easily frightened by a person wearing a mask."

Garrison hardly slept. After rescuing animals all day, she would toil most of the night, creating work assignments for the volunteers. Using a large map of the city that she broke down into small gridlike sections, she determined where to send each team the next day. Then she would catch a few hours of shut-eye in the front seat of her car. The stress and loss of sleep caused her to lose her voice. For the daily 5:30 A.M. volunteer meetings, she often needed to relay her instructions to someone else who would shout them out to the teams.

With an ever-enlarging corps of rescuers scouring the flooded city, the number of saved pets increased from a few dozen a day to several hundred a day. Some evenings the number of animal-filled vehicles that lined up to enter Lamar Dixon stretched for a quarter mile, causing the volunteers to wait four or five hours before checking in the rescued pets.

At the bustling shelter, veterinarians were hooking up animals to IVs and treating them for dehydration and upper respiratory infections. Many cats that hadn't eaten for days slipped into a medical condition that made them reject food, so the vets had to use feeding tubes to get the pets' systems jump-started.

Meanwhile, back in the city, Garrison and her rescue partner, Drew Moore, crawled under houses, broke into apartments, and climbed onto roofs to rescue animals. The duo was saving the lives of about 50 pets a day, including birds, hamsters, fish, ferrets, chinchillas, turtles, guinea pigs, and rabbits. Garrison treated every animal the same, because she knew it was someone's beloved pet, someone's family member. If the birds were in a cage, they were brought to Lamar Dixon. For other pet birds, Garrison opened the window and let them outside, where their odds of surviving were greater.

One day, while passing by an apartment building, Garrison heard panicky meowing. She looked up. There, plastered against a third-floor window, was a cat staring at her and yowling for help. Garrison charged into the building and broke into the apartment, where the grateful feline leaped into her arms and began purring wildly. A thorough search of the apartment revealed a second cat. "Good for you, kitty," Garrison said to the first cat. "You made enough noise to save yourself and your friend."

Nearing the end of the second week, Garrison and Moore arrived in a neighborhood where the floodwaters had yet to recede. It was quiet—until several National Guard armored tanklike vehicles rolled through the water. Somewhere nearby, dogs were barking.

"It's amazing we're still hearing dogs," she told Drew. "We need to find them and rescue them. I'm going to get us a tank."

"You're kidding," Moore said.

"No, I'm serious. We've been saving the animals that we can reach, but there are animals still alive that we haven't been able to reach. Those dogs are calling to us, so I'm getting us a tank."

As the youngest of six kids in her family, Garrison learned at an early age how to be assertive. She waded over to a group of National Guardsmen, who were in an armored vehicle. "Hey, you guys," she hailed them. "You've got to help me. I need you to take me to where the dogs are barking nonstop. It's just for a couple of hours." She wasn't taking no for an answer, and eventually they agreed to help.

The Guardsmen drove Garrison and Moore through 4-foot-deep water to the block where she heard the barking. Suddenly, she spotted a fawn-colored bullmastiff—a large breed with a solid build and short snout—on the roof of a flooded house. Typically, a dog like that weighs about 120 pounds, but this one was skin and bones. He stared directly at Garrison, and her eyes connected with his. *He wants to be saved*, she thought.

"We've got to stop and rescue that dog," she told the Guardsmen. "Move as close to the house as you can." The vehicle lumbered into position, allowing her to crawl through a window. As she reached the stairs to the second floor, she found a handwritten sign that said MY DOG'S NAME IS BLAKE. PLEASE SAVE HIM. I ALSO HAVE A CAT. The owner had written his phone number at the bottom. *I never would have known there's a cat in the house*, Garrison thought.

Her top priority was to save the dog. She reached the attic but couldn't find a way out onto the roof. *How in the world did the dog get out there?* she wondered. She managed to pull an air-conditioning unit out of a wall to create an opening. Seconds later, Blake squeezed through. Whining from happiness, he licked her face and wagged his tail. "Oh, you're so skinny," Garrison told him. "There's no way you should have been able to survive on this roof for seventeen days. Clearly, Blake, you didn't read the textbook that says you should be dead by now." Then she searched for, and found, the cat.

Blake and his feline friend were taken to Lamar Dixon for medical treatment, because the animals were severely dehydrated and the dog was about 50 pounds underweight. Garrison called the owner with the good news that the pets were safe and recovering. The owner wept with joy because he had feared they had perished. Blake never forgot his rescuer: Each time Garrison checked on him at Lamar Dixon, he greeted her with sloppy kisses.

Every day, Garrison teetered back and forth emotionally—from joy over saving a dog locked in a bathroom to heartache over finding three kittens trying to nurse on the body of their lifeless mother. Seeing those starving kitties and their dead mama on the front porch of a house after discovering 11 dead cats outside another home put Garrison over the edge. She sobbed until her gut hurt.

When she recovered from her crying jag, she realized that they were outdoor cats that had been fed by their owners before the hurricane but now had no food source. More and more, she was spotting strays and abandoned pets sitting helplessly on small islands of high ground, porches, car roofs, and other large objects. With each passing day, these animals were looking worse and wasting away.

At Lamar Dixon, Garrison told authorities, "We should set up food and water stations throughout the neighborhoods for the strays." At first, officials were reluctant because they worried the food stations would attract rats and other vermin. But Garrison won out, so she assigned teams to place open bags of food and containers of clean water at specific locations throughout the neighborhoods. That way, she hoped, the animals might live long enough to get rescued.

A few weeks into the rescue operation came distressing news: Officials announced that volunteers couldn't bring any more animals into Lamar Dixon because the facility had run out of space and cages. Authorities declined to transport the animals out of state for fostering because they were worried the move would make it more difficult for owners to reunite with their pets. The only new animals allowed into Lamar Dixon were ones in critical condition.

Refusing to stop their mission, Garrison and her teams continued to break into houses of people on the list wanting their pets saved. In homes where the animals were still alive, the volunteers left bowls of food and water. Then they spray-painted a notice on the outside that said something like DOG INSIDE F/W or 2 CATS INSIDE F/W, indicating that food and water had been left for them. When state officials lifted the ban on sending rescued pets to out-of-state shelters, Garrison's teams went back to the houses to retrieve the animals they couldn't take earlier.

But Garrison knew she and the volunteers were running out of time. *There's only so long an animal can live without food and water, and there are so many more that haven't been reached.*

By now, in many houses that had been flooded, she was finding paw prints in the mud and sludge and then discovering the animal's body. She sometimes found deep scratch marks on the inside of front or back doors in the house of a dead dog. Those were telltale signs that many animals didn't die during the hurricane or drown in the flood. They had survived by jumping onto tables and counters or getting to a higher floor. Tragically, they died because rescuers couldn't reach them in time. "We don't have enough people to break into homes and rescue the animals," she told her partner, Moore. "The pets are dying of starvation and dehydration. This is one of the hardest things for me to live with."

One day, during the fourth week, she was on a street where the flood levels had dropped considerably. She went into a house and found a dead cat curled on top of a china cabinet. Judging from the waterline left on the cabinet, the flood had reached almost to the top. The sad sight triggered another emotional moment for Garrison. *I can only imagine the fear and suffering that cat endured. To be stuck up there and die, because it had no food and no water . . .* She wept.

To do her job effectively, Garrison had to stay focused and keep her emotions in check. But it wasn't easy, not when she found the bodies of dogs that had been chained to front porches or bodies of cats left in crates. They didn't stand a chance. Garrison knew if she gave in to her emotions, she would be useless. She worked fast and furiously so she didn't have time to dwell on the sad scenes she encountered. For most volunteers, tears often flowed on the hour drive from the city to Lamar Dixon when they had time to reflect on what they had seen.

Often, after entering a house, she would take a breath and know instantly that she was too late. The place would reek of death. And it wasn't always from a dead pet. Sometimes it was its owner. Garrison once came across the body of an elderly woman on the front porch. The body was partially covered with a blanket.

Another time, a man called Garrison and said he hadn't been able to reach his 80-year-old father. "I'm sure my dad is all right and got out, but his dog—who's everything to him—was probably left behind, and not by my dad's choice. Could you please send someone to rescue the dog?"

Garrison assigned one of the volunteers to go to the address. The rescuer broke into the house and found the dog was alive, but the owner—who hadn't evacuated after all—was dead. Garrison later offered condolences to the man's son. "That would be just like my dad," the son said. "He wouldn't abandon his dog."

"It's so sad," Garrison said. "People died unnecessarily because they refused to leave their animals."

Among those who had hunkered down in their homes during the storm were Luana Maria Rathman and Margie Wilmoth. They chose to stay with their ten cats, four dogs, and a rabbit. After the levees broke and flooded their neighborhood, the women reluctantly evacuated by helicopter, taking only their Chihuahua and their smallest cat. Before leaving, the owners left behind fresh water and open 50-pound bags of food for their pets, and also knocked a hole in the back door so the cats could go in and out. As the women were hoisted into the helicopter, they could hear their cats yowling in terror. The distraught owners ended up in a shelter in Texas, having no idea of the fate of the animals they left behind.

Days later, a film crew from Animal Planet followed Garrison and Moore on several rescues, including to Rathman and Wilmoth's house. In the backyard were three big dogs—a Newfoundland, a Doberman mix, and a German shepherd mix—that looked confused and ragged. Garrison and Moore managed to rescue two of the dogs, as well as the women's rabbit, but the Newfoundland scurried into a crawl space under the house. The three animals were taken to Lamar Dixon.

Shortly afterward, Animal Planet aired a preview of a special program about the Katrina pet rescues that showed Garrison, Moore, and the two dogs. A friend of the owners was watching Animal Planet and recognized their dogs, so she alerted the women, who contacted the cable network.

They were eventually reunited with the two dogs and rabbit. When Rathman and Wilmoth finally returned to repair their damaged house, they found eight of the cats had survived. So, too, had Yeti, the Newfoundland that had refused to be rescued. The dog had faithfully been guarding the house all these weeks. She survived, because Garrison and volunteers had been leaving extra food and water for her.

One of Garrison's worst days occurred near the end of September. She and a friend had entered 25 houses—and in every house, they discovered they were too late. At the last home, the pair plopped on the front steps and bawled. Garrison felt so defeated. "We just couldn't reach them in time . . ." She sobbed. "I'm having a real hard time dealing with that."

Adding to her despair, authorities announced that October 1 was the deadline for state-sanctioned rescues. After that date, there would be no more. "This is crazy!" Garrison told officials. "We've been rescuing three hundred to four hundred animals a day inside houses. These aren't stray animals I'm talking about. These are pets locked in houses."

"But that was early on in the rescue effort," a state veterinarian told her. "The numbers have dropped significantly since then. After nearly five weeks, there's no chance that animals are still alive."

"You're wrong," Garrison declared. "We're still bringing in animals every night. In fact, I'll have my people bring the animals to your office at the end of the day so you can see for yourself."

Early on the morning of October 1, Garrison called a meeting of the volunteers. She stood on a golf cart and, although her voice was hoarse, addressed the crowd: "The state is saying no more rescues starting today. Well, I am not leaving. And if you want to stay with me, and you want to continue rescuing animals with me, we can be a strong force."

All vowed to keep working. Best Friends Animal Society opened up a temporary facility in nearby Metairie and took in hundreds more animals after the deadline. Garrison cofounded a new nonprofit called Animal Rescue New Orleans (ARNO), which replenished food stations for strays and abandoned pets.

After working tirelessly for six weeks nonstop, Garrison was on the brink of total exhaustion and needed to return home. On the drive back to Charleston, she relived the good moments and the bad ones. Even though she had given her body and soul to the cause, she wished she could have done more. Still, she took comfort in her successes, knowing rescued pets helped the healing process for their owners, many of whom lost everything.

In the scale of all the human suffering in the ravaged region, the plight of pets might seem trivial to some people, but not to anyone who ever loved a dog or a cat. And certainly not to Jane Garrison.

At the Humane Society of the United States' 2006 Genesis Awards, Garrison was honored for personally rescuing 1,200 animals in six weeks.

Animal-welfare groups and volunteers such as Garrison who rushed to the New Orleans area are credited with saving more than 15,000 animals victimized by Hurricane Katrina. Only about 20 percent of the pets were eventually reunited with their owners. Many other pets were adopted or cared for in foster homes and shelters. No one knows how many pets and strays were killed by the storm, but it's estimated to be in the tens of thousands.

Many people died or suffered needlessly, because authorities wouldn't let them evacuate with their pets. According to a poll of residents conducted after the storm, 44 percent of those who chose to ride out the storm did so solely to remain with their pets. State and federal officials have, in many cases, changed their policy that banned pets in emergency shelters and evacuation buses and now accept families with their animals. Also, disaster animal-response teams have been set up to coordinate with government officials in emergency situations.

"Animals are part of the family," says Garrison. "You don't ever want to leave a family member behind in a disaster. What happened in New Orleans was a hard lesson for the country to learn. We won't make that mistake again."

Today, Garrison, who lives in California with her husband and their four rescue cats and two rescue dogs, continues to advocate for animals. "I have such a strong passion to help animals," she says. "It's so deep within me that it's a part of who I am. I can never turn my back to a suffering animal without doing something."

"I CAN'T LET THE PEOPLE DOWN"

Brice Phillips

Exposed to Hurricane Katrina's wicked gusts that were trying to whip him free from his tight grip, Brice Phillips slowly continued his dangerous climb up a swaying 60-foot emergency operations center radio tower. He wished he were someplace else. But he volunteered to scale the rickety structure because he knew people were depending on him—first responders, disaster officials, and, most important, his fellow survivors.

His radio station—the only link to the outside world from a county smashed to smithereens by the killer storm—had been knocked off the air by the wind-driven rain. A vital cable connection to a transmitter was compromised. It was up to the shaggy-haired, slender 39-year-old radio whiz to repair the damage.

Failure meant a total loss of life-saving communications. No reports from the area's emergency-management team. No messages to and from police, fire, and FEMA authorities. No information to the people who needed it most to survive.

Phillips ignored the negative thinking just as he ignored the devastating storm surge below that was thrusting everything in its path out toward the Gulf. And so, as the whistling gusts slapped him from all sides, he continued his climb up the wobbly tower. *I have to fix this*, he told himself. *I will fix this.*

Trained in television and radio production and repair, Phillips lived in the quaint beachfront town of Bay St. Louis, Mississippi, population 8,000. Located 60 miles northeast of New Orleans, the seaside retreat of picturesque frame houses was considered by tourists as a jewel of the Mississippi Gulf Coast.

But it was (and still is) a bull's-eye for destructive tropical storms and deadly hurricanes, especially Camille in 1969, one of the most powerful hurricanes ever to slam into the United States. Camille flattened and drowned much of Bay St. Louis and killed 137 people in Mississippi.

Several years before Katrina, Phillips wanted to create an amateur radio-based broadcast station that would act as a public service for the community as well as provide emergency communications for police and fire departments in disaster situations. The idea was spawned during his days as a teenager when, following storms and floods, he rode around on a ten-speed bike equipped with a battery-powered CB radio that he operated to connect storm victims with local government agencies and resources.

In 2002, Phillips and his girlfriend, Christine Stach, who, like him, was a licensed amateur radio operator, laid the groundwork for a unique station. With boundless determination and little money, they made their dream come true. Phillips collected used and discarded equipment that he repaired. He poured the concrete for the pad of his tiny studio and the 130-foot tower that was erected next to his modest house. Stach created the programming, lined up local musicians for live performances, and organized her massive collection of 6,000 CDs.

In January 2003, after the Federal Communications Commission granted their nonprofit organization a low-power FM license, amateur broadcast radio station WQRZ went on the air. (QRZ is ham-radio lingo for "who is calling?")

The station was the first of its kind in the nation, not bad for two financially strapped people who also lived with serious disabilities. Phillips was diagnosed with a chronic neurochemical disorder known as adult ADHD, short for attention deficit/hyperactivity disorder. It's a condition known to cause depression, mood swings, anxiety, and lack of concentration and organization. Stach required a wheelchair at times after contracting multiple sclerosis, a progressive disease that affects the central nervous system and causes problems with muscle control, vision, and balance.

But they refused to let their disabilities stifle their commitment to WQRZ, a quirky station that gained a loyal audience in its tight broadcast area in Hancock County, which included the towns of Bay St. Louis, Waveland, Kiln, Pearlington, and Diamondhead. Their station served 17,460 households and more than 39,000 individuals along the western

Mississippi shore. Listeners loved the programming mix of blues on Tuesday, world music on Wednesday, jazz on Thursday, rock on Friday, and New Age on weekends, along with call-in shows, live musical programs, and interviews with local officials and characters. As on-air personalities, Phillips and Stach were well-known throughout the community. His ADHD was no secret to listeners, because he freely talked about it, adding, "It's not a disability. It's an ability."

Because WQRZ was licensed as a commercial-free, educational broadcast station, it operated on a shoestring budget that relied on volunteers and donations and whatever money Phillips and Stach could spare from their Social Security disability checks. Always in the back of Phillips's mind was the belief that WQRZ would play a major role during the next disaster.

That moment arrived when hurricane warnings went up along the Gulf Coast region for Katrina. As a navy brat who spent part of his childhood in Taiwan, Phillips knew firsthand the destructive force of typhoons—and Katrina was forecast to be more powerful than anything he had ever experienced. The hurricane was generating waves 40 to 60 feet high off the mouth of the Mississippi River and was expected to create a storm surge of at least 30 feet when it reached Bay St. Louis.

Realizing he wouldn't be able to broadcast from his house, which stood only 14 feet above sea level, Phillips decided to move his operation to the county's emergency operations center (EOC), a cinder-block building next to the courthouse, which was 28 feet above sea level.

Climbing his tower in blustery winds on Sunday afternoon, he removed an antenna and transmitter. He gathered other equipment, including wires, cables, solar panels, and laptops, and brought them in his old Chevy van to the EOC. Despite increasing winds and rain, he climbed the EOC's 60-foot tower and rigged the antenna and transmitter. WQRZ was off the air for four hours during the transfer of equipment. When the station was up and running again around 5 P.M., it began broadcasting, between songs, a prerecorded message for people to evacuate. It aired mostly New Age, light rock, and folk music, because Phillips and Stach hoped the playlist would help calm listeners at this stressful time.

During their last-minute move, the couple had collected important papers from their house and put them in tote bags, which were stuffed in the back of the van. Other possessions in the home were placed on top of shelves and tall furniture. The couple also packed an old sedan, a Ford Crown Victoria, with clothes, other items, and Stach's longhaired dachshund, Killer. The dog wasn't allowed in the EOC, so he had to stay in the car.

The building was initially occupied by about 50 people, including county officials, FEMA representatives, volunteers, firefighters, and Mississippi National Guardsmen. When forecasters projected the hurricane would roar right over Bay St. Louis with winds of 125 miles an hour and a 30-foot storm surge, FEMA and the Guard decided to evacuate and urged the others to do the same.

Brian "Hootie" Adam, the head of the Hancock County

Emergency Management Agency, announced, "I am not leaving the people of this county. My job is to help them in precisely this kind of situation, and I can't do that if I relocate somewhere else."

"You need to get out now," said a FEMA official. "It's not safe here."

"Everyone is free to go," Adam said, "but who is staying with me?"

His four staff members along with firefighters and volunteers stood up. So did Phillips and Stach. "I can't leave," Phillips told the others. "I've got to stay with Hootie. Without the tools and communication that I know how to use, he's toast."

Before leaving, a National Guard officer said bluntly, "You realize you're all going to die here."

With every passing hour throughout the night, the terror intensified for the 35 people who remained behind. As the center of the hurricane drew closer, the incredibly low air pressure caused everyone's ears to pop. The shrieking wind blew so hard it nearly ripped a door off its hinges, prompting the occupants to lash the door with bungee cords to keep it from flying off. The roof creaked and groaned as if it would break apart at any second. Ceiling tiles and insulation tumbled to the floor and power flickered on and off.

And then water started coming in through the back of the EOC—supposedly the safest place in the building. *We're at 28 feet above sea level and there's water outside?* Phillips said to himself. *This is spooky and definitely scary.*

Phillips and the others rescued the phones, equipment, and computers in the back room by putting them in higher places in the besieged building.

Joel Ellzie, emergency operations coordinator, was manning one of the phones. While standing in 18 inches of water, he received a call with grim news: The worst was yet to come for Bay St. Louis. Then all the land lines went dead. Cell phones and satellite phones no longer worked, either. When the region's power grid fell victim to the hurricane, the EOC's generator kicked in.

At regular intervals, WQRZ was relaying information from a National Weather Service computer that was transmitting the current position of the hurricane and giving bulletins warning everyone in its path to move to higher ground.

But those inside the EOC stayed put. Recognizing the possibility of ending up dead just as the officer had warned, they chose to make it easy for their bodies to be identified. First, they counted off from 1 to 35. Whatever number each person had was written on a sheet of paper beside his or her name. Phillips was number 12; Stach was 8. After the list was completed, the sheet was slipped into a plastic re-sealable food storage bag and nailed to the ceiling. They also used a water-proof marker pen to write their number on their arm. There was some small comfort—although quite unsettling—thinking that if they drowned, at least others would know who had sacrificed his or her life in service to the community.

At first light on Monday, Phillips was alarmed by the storm surge rushing across the parking lot—and rising rapidly. The winds were so fierce that pebbles from the EOC's stone-and-asphalt flat roof were blowing off and crashing into windows and windshields of every vehicle in the parking lot, except Phillips' van and car.

But the van didn't escape damage. Before the storm, he had secured a ladder and an antenna lengthwise on top of the vehicle. When Katrina reached its peak wind velocity, a violent gust swept under the equipment and lifted it, which peeled back the roof of his van.

"When is this water going to stop rising?" Phillips asked no one in particular. "People are going to get washed away and die out there." Watching airborne debris zip past the building, he added, "Anyone crazy enough to go out in this storm will likely get his head knocked off from flying objects."

Later that morning, as the surge flooded the vehicles in the parking lot, the water shorted out the electrical wiring of several cars, causing engines to start and lights to go on.

"Hey," shouted someone who was staring out the window. "There's a car on fire!"

Phillips walked over to the window and gasped. "Oh my God! That's my car!" Its alarm system was blaring, and its headlights were flashing as smoked filled the inside.

Stach screamed, "The dog is in there! Someone save Killer!"

Phillips and two volunteer firemen wrestled the EOC door open and then waded out into the treacherous wind and storm surge. Pounded by the rain and merciless gusts, Phillips reached the car, opened the hood, and yanked the electrical connections from the battery that had caused the fire. The wires were so hot they scorched his hands.

Meanwhile, the firefighters were trying to put out the smoldering fire inside the car, which was belching thick black smoke. "I can't see the dog!" yelled one fireman as he sprayed the interior with a fire extinguisher. Phillips went to help but he couldn't find the black-and-tan dog, either.

Believing that Killer was dead from smoke inhalation or had tumbled out of the flooded car and been swept away, Phillips hurriedly trudged through the water to check on Stach in the EOC. He was worried that the emotional trauma caused by the unknown fate of her cherished pet had triggered a bad physical response in her body.

Inside, he found Stach in the throes of a serious multiple-sclerosis attack. She was experiencing involuntary muscle movement, especially in her hands. Her head jerking left and right and her mouth drooling, she was able to utter through slurred speech, "My legs won't move."

Phillips threw his arms around Stach and tried to calm her down. But there wasn't much he could say that could soothe her, not when it meant telling her that Killer was dead. Although he had spent much of the last two and a half years ad-libbing into a microphone, he now found it hard to find the right words. He was hurting, too, from seeing the physical and mental torture that his girlfriend was suffering—never mind that they were enduring a brutal hurricane in a building that could potentially become their watery tomb.

An emergency medical technician who was in the EOC was monitoring Stach's vital signs when firefighter Wade Hicks burst into the room, clutching something in his arms. "I found the dog!" he announced. "Killer is alive!"

"God bless you, man!" Phillips shouted.

Hicks handed the soot-covered dog to Stach, who burst into tears and needed another ten minutes to calm herself and regain control of her MS-afflicted body.

Before Phillips had time to savor his relief over seeing that Stach and the dog would be all right, the EOC's generator died. The storm surge had swamped it, knocking the radio broadcast off the air. But Phillips was prepared for such an occurrence. He hooked the necessary equipment, CD disc changer, and transmitter to several car batteries that he had brought with him. Soon WQRZ was once again playing New Age music and relaying weather updates.

But 20 minutes later, as Katrina headed northeast, the broadcast went silent once again. "Why is this happening?" Adam asked.

Perplexed, Phillips examined his equipment, trying to find the cause. He figured it out in no time. "In my haste to get the antenna up outside the EOC before the hurricane hit, I didn't put waterproof tape on the connection of the coaxial cable," he explained. "The back-side winds drove the rain in between the connection, and that's why we lost transmission."

Adam knew the answer to the next question but asked anyway: "How do you fix it?"

"I'll have to climb the tower, get the water out of the coaxial cable, and put tape around the connection," Phillips replied.

"It's way too dangerous," Adam said. "Don't go, at least not now. It's still blowing pretty hard."

"I can't wait," Phillips said. "I need to get back on the air. People's lives are dependent on the information we give them. "

Adam again urged him not to attempt the repairs, but Phillips ignored him. "It's my fault we're off the air, and I'm going to fix it," Phillips declared. After strapping on a helmet, he grabbed what he needed and promised everyone, "I'll be careful."

He pushed the back door open and slogged through the surge, which had switched directions and was now flowing back toward the Gulf. Although the winds had slackened a bit by this time, hurricane-force gusts were still blowing at up to 80 miles an hour—hardly ideal for someone climbing a 60-foot tower.

Phillips reached the base of the tower, which was swaying in the wind, and looked up. *I can't let the people down. I have to do this or we'll remain off the air,* he told himself. *Just don't do anything stupid and don't rush it.*

He secured a safety harness to a sturdy leather belt around his waist and then attached it to the tower. Tightly gripping each rung, he slowly inched his way up. One step up . . . stop . . . one step up . . . stop. Phillips was less concerned about getting blown off than he was about the tower toppling over, because it was shaky and affixed to a flimsy metal addition built on to the back of the EOC building.

About halfway up, he paused and looked around at the unbelievable scene. All he could see was water—no dry ground anywhere. The storm surge's strong current was carrying away rubble from smashed houses, uprooted trees, and flooded vehicles out to the Gulf. At least the water level was falling rapidly. Scanning the distance in the direction of his home, he saw nothing but devastation. *My house is probably gone*, he told himself. But he didn't dwell on his loss. *Everyone is counting on me to get the broadcast back on the air.*

And so he climbed. The higher he went, the more the tower rocked back and forth. He wasn't afraid of heights, but the wobbling motion made him seasick. Still, he kept scaling the structure. One step up . . . stop . . . one step up . . . stop. It took him 90 arduous minutes to reach the top, get the water out of the connection to the coaxial cable, and weatherproof it. He then climbed down safely.

After being silenced for more than two hours, WQRZ was transmitting crucial information once again.

About an hour after Phillips completed his tower-of-terror excursion, he stood with several firefighters outside on the front steps of the EOC building, which was now above the waterline. Although the flood was receding, it remained too dangerous to drive, because the water was deep in many places, and the current was still powerful enough to shove a vehicle off the road.

To the men's surprise, they saw a Suburban—a large SUV—motoring past them about 100 yards away. When the vehicle reached a dip in the flooded road, the current began carrying it off. Inside the Suburban was a family of six, who yelled for help.

Phillips and the firefighters grabbed ropes and life jackets and waded out into the hazardous water to rescue the people and bring them back inside the EOC.

Later that afternoon, when it was deemed somewhat safe, Phillips ventured out with several first responders in a jacked-up four-wheel-drive truck. Wherever they looked, they saw total destruction. The storm surge had destroyed most everything from the beach to the first nine blocks inland. Only concrete pilings were left of beachfront stilt houses. Charmingly painted residences had been reduced to colorful splinters. On Main Street, buildings that were still standing were filled with sand, silt, and debris that came in through broken windows and blown-out doorways. Overturned cars and downed trees stripped of leaves blocked side streets.

The men drove along the main drag, Highway 90, toward the bay to check on the 2-mile-long bridge that connected Bay St. Louis with the beach town of Pass Christian. But the bridge's entire roadway was washed away. All that remained were the concrete stanchions that had supported the four-lane span for the previous fifty years.

When they returned to the EOC, Phillips went on the air for his first live broadcast since Katrina struck. He told his listeners that the Bay Bridge was gone and that everyone in the EOC was okay. "If you have a medical emergency, try to get someone to bring you to the EOC," he said. "We have people here who can help you. Or tie something red on your front door so when search and rescue starts, they'll get to you as quickly as possible with the limited resources we have."

Phillips's voice was the first one heard at ground zero along the Gulf Coast. In fact, of the 41 radio stations from New Orleans to Mobile, Alabama, WQRZ was one of only four still broadcasting.

"Survivors, please get to the EOC and check in so we know you are okay," he told listeners. "We need to get a head-count of who has survived. To find help, make it to the highway, because that's the first road being cleared. The only shelter available is at the Bay High School gym, but food and water supplies are extremely low."

On Tuesday, the day after the storm, Phillips went out again so he could give listeners a firsthand report of the horrific damage. Coffins from the cemetery were strewn on front lawns. Beached boats were resting on their sides in parking lots and drive-throughs. Many houses had been lifted off their foundations and shoved into the middle of streets. Bodies of people and animals lay in ditches. People were stumbling through the rubble in a stupor, trying to cope with a community in ruins. Some had shopping carts, breaking into stores for food, clothing, and water. *This is worse than a war zone*, he thought. *The destruction is so overwhelming. Who is still alive? Who is left?*

After the third day, Phillips chose not to go out anymore. It hurt too much. Besides, his role was to keep communications going. *I have to stay true to my mission*, he thought. *It's my world. I am the only one with the capability here.*

With the blessing of the manager of the area's only RadioShack—which had 12 feet of water in the building during the storm—Phillips earlier rode in a fire truck to the store and gathered cables and other radio gear that he needed to create an emergency communications network at the EOC. After helping get the generator operating again, he strung 21 antennas on the tower and damaged roof of the EOC. He used downed flag poles and anything else he could find to make antennas, setting up a system so the team could communicate without phone lines, Internet, or wireless hookup. While keeping the radio station on the air, Phillips and Stach and volunteers routed ambulance and emergency calls around the clock, using ham radios, some of which he rigged with jumper cables and car batteries.

WQRZ and Phillips's ham-radio operation were the only daily sources of information for survivors in the tents, trailers, and bashed homes in Hancock County. The National Guard didn't arrive until four days after the storm, and military helicopters appeared a day after that.

Hancock County was on its own, so it was up to Phillips to tell fellow survivors the locations for the distribution of food, water, ice, clothing, and bare necessities as well as for shelters and medical care.

Recognizing the important role that WQRZ was doing for the community, FEMA delivered 3,500 battery-operated radios that were passed out to survivors so they could listen to the daily bulletins and other important information that Phillips was reporting.

Over the next several weeks, WQRZ helped keep the county together. Phillips's familiar baritone voice brought a sense of comfort to listeners who were told when and where the buses were running; where and how to apply for small business loans, FEMA assistance, and emergency blue roof tarps; where to find wireless Internet access; what restaurants, stores, and services had reopened. Stach's music was a welcome relief for survivors whose ears were assaulted daily by the din of heavy equipment and chain saws.

Phillips helped people in Hancock County contact their relatives across the nation. He was in touch with other ham operators, passing messages back and forth so survivors could let family and friends know who was safe in the stricken area. The messages, like the following one, were broadcast over the radio: "It's to Sister Claudia Murphy, St. Catherine Village, Madison, Mississippi: 'Pray. Know that Rod, Dot, Margaret, and George are okay. We lost Nan, God rest her soul. Pearlington was leveled. Jane and I were in deep water for hours. Rod had lots of water, too. Haven't talked with him, but we heard he was okay. Devastation is surreal. Love you very much. Will call as soon as I can. Pray, pray, pray. Love, Jan Murphy.'"

The hardest part for Phillips about broadcasting regular updates was reading the list of those in the county who were still missing since Hurricane Katrina had made landfall. (The death toll in the county eventually would reach 51.)

With only a few hours of sleep a night, he was handling dispatches between agencies and departments, broadcasting public service announcements, interviewing officials, and restoring original equipment of the county's radio system for the police and fire departments. "This is why ADHD is a benefit, because when multi-tasking is required, I excel," he boasted to his audience. He was also salvaging flooded computers, opening them up, drying them out, and getting them to work again.

Although the couple's home was destroyed, the radio station's tower and the 8-foot-by-8-foot transmission shed remained standing. Eventually, with the help of volunteers, the temporary radio setup at the EOC was transferred back to the original site where it broadcast with a stronger signal. Phillips and Stach were able to move into a FEMA trailer on the property, because the house was damaged beyond repair.

Three weeks after Katrina, the weary survivors of Hancock County were pummeled by another killer hurricane, this one named Rita, which whacked the Gulf Coast, spawning tornadoes and floods. During the height of the storm, Phillips was broadcasting from the EOC, warning residents of a possible twister, when a fire alarm sounded in the building from a short-circuited machine. Everyone was ordered to evacuate, but he refused to leave his post and continued to broadcast.

When a blackout knocked WQRZ off the air, its generator needed to be started up. However, floodwaters prevented easy access to the transmitter site to refuel the generator. Knowing that listeners were relying on him for crucial updates, Phillips refused to wait for the water level to recede. Even though he was sick and weak from lack of sleep since Katrina, he jumped into the toxic water and waded for several hundred strenuous yards while floating ten gallons of diesel fuel with him. When he reached the generator, he filled it and started it so the radio station could broadcast again. Then he returned to the microphone.

But he was losing his voice and his energy. Forcing himself to see a doctor, Phillips was diagnosed with bronchitis and pneumonia and ordered to remain in bed. After a week of recovery, Phillips returned to his favorite place in the world— in front of the microphone in his little broadcast booth, trying to make lives better for the good people of Hancock County.

In 2006, Phillips went to Washington, D.C., to receive the Small Business Administration's esteemed Phoenix Award for outstanding contributions to disaster recovery by a volunteer. The award was presented to him by President George W. Bush.

"It was extremely important that my parents were there to see it," Phillips says. "My mom had just been diagnosed with Alzheimer's disease, but she understood what the award meant to me. All I could do during the ceremony was thank my folks. I was blessed that they had adopted me and stood by me even though I had given

them a hard time growing up because of a disability that none of us knew I had. I was proud that my parents saw that I had accomplished something with my life."

In August 2008, winds and water from Hurricane Gustav hit Hancock County and flooded WQRZ's broadcast shed. Despite the damage, Phillips continued to fulfill his mission of providing emergency information to the community—by broadcasting out in the open from his porch. Two months later, volunteers, including a group known as the Giving Circle, Inc., finished construction of a new transmission shed and studio for WQRZ.

Four years later, in August 2012, Hurricane Isaac barreled into the county, flooding the station's studio. When the water was knee-deep inside, Phillips contacted authorities, who rescued three volunteer staff members. But true to form, he stayed behind and continued to broadcast emergency information to listeners. "I'm not going to leave what protects this community," he told a reporter at the time.

Today, he and Christine Stach continue to run WQRZ, which can be heard online at katrinaradio.com. They've spent every available cent of their modest income and donations from contributors to keep the station on the air. As of 2015, they still lived in the RV next to the transmission shed.

"I'm going to keep doing this until I go flat broke," Phillips declares, "because WQRZ is a community radio that has helped not only change lives but save lives."